AN ENGLISH FLAVOUR

RECIPES FROM HOPE END

Patricia Hegarty

Illustrated by Crispin Thornton-Jones
with photographs by Jacqui Hirst

BOXTREE

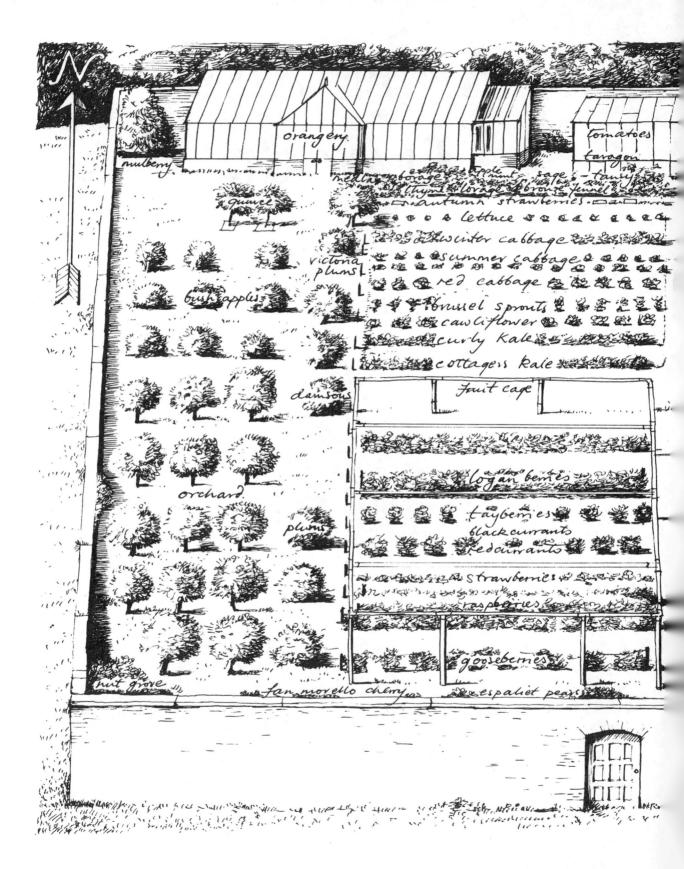

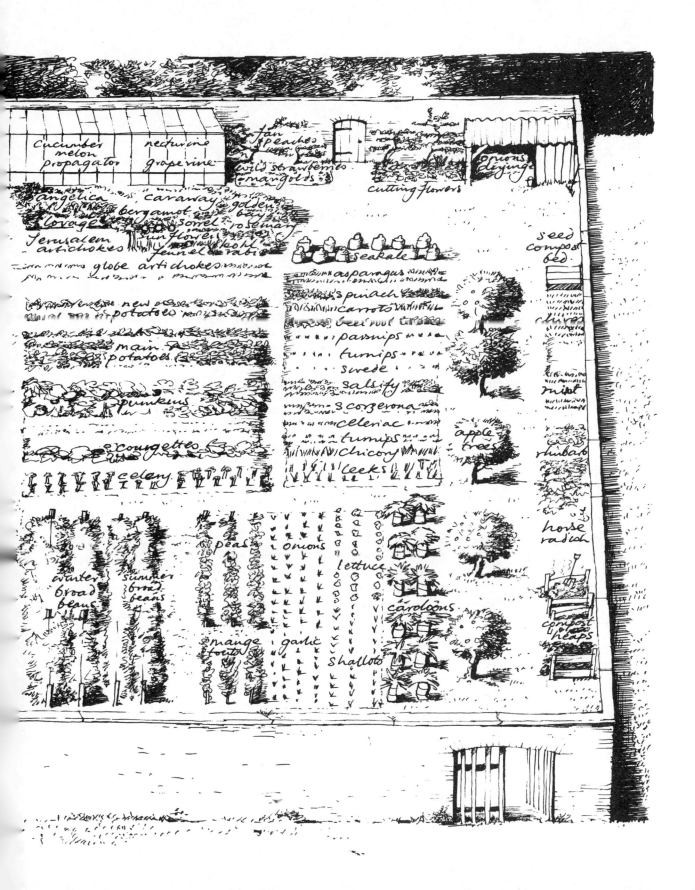

All our life is the continuation of tradition, a process of creative reinterpretation and a movement from sign to sign in which we can conceive neither beginning nor end.

- Don Cupitt, *The Long Legged Fly*

First published in Great Britain in 1988 by Equation
This edition published in 1996 by Boxtree Limited

Text © Patricia Hegarty 1988
Illustrations © Crispin Thornton-Jones 1988
Photographs © Jacqui Hurst 1996

The right of Patricia Hegarty to be identified as Author of this Work has been asserted by her
in accordance with the Copyright, Designs and Patents Act 1988.

10 9 8 7 6 5 4 3 2 1

Designed by Bradbury & Williams
Printed and bound in Great Britain by The Bath Press, Bath

Boxtree Limited
Broadwall House
21 Broadwall
London SE1 9PL

A CIP catalogue entry for this book is available from the British Library.

ISBN 0 7522 1053 X

FOREWORD

Patricia Hegarty is a rare bird among the flock of food professionals in England since she is, by birth and nurture, a truly regional cook. She works where she has lived all her life, in Herefordshire, at Hope End, a romantic house with minarets and arches and a courtyard, a house poised on a sloping dip of parkland where Elizabeth Barrett Browning passed much of her youth. Mrs Hegarty's family has for six centuries lived in this part of the country. Many of them have been connected with the production of food, having been vinegar makers, fruit farmers and canners, chutney and jam makers.

This rootedness is unusual in England which has seen for a long time now the movement of people away from their country origins. The restlessness has deprived us of that stability still treasured by, for instance, the Italians and French, of belonging to a particular region, and to a particular small town or village in it. 'Mon pays' calls back the French of all classes at weekends, festivals, for the long summer holiday; the possession of a second home there, whether it be a fishing shack on the river or a cottage on the farm or estate, seems to be the aim of a majority of town dwellers. This means that regional tastes in food survive; they adapt rather than drown under urban or even wider influence.

Patricia Hegarty's style and her understanding of local food has been reinforced by her marriage. John Hegarty, who was a reluctant solicitor when they met, was born in China but grew up in Surrey during the war where he roamed the countryside in a perfect freedom that we dare not allow our children today. He has long belonged to the Soil Association: and always been accustomed to the aims of organic gardening and farming which was until more recently than we sometimes realize the normal way, and the experience of a more numerous repertoire of fruit, vegetables and herbs than most people now are familiar with. He knew that quiet world of rectories, large farms, manor houses where the style of cooking has gently meandered along in a direct line from Eliza Acton, unmoved by fashion except where it could be fitted in smoothly, responding more to the excitements of the seed catalogue than to either the grandeur of chefs or the depredations of mass-food industry, taking the good things of a well-tended countryside as a matter of course.

To her knowledge of the regional style, and the classic French style which inevitably underpins our best food, Patricia Hegarty has added a knack of improving the familiar with an unusual ingredient that makes all the difference, without affecting its essential character. She sets off the magnificent, properly hung Hereford beef with tarragon or savory or a cider sauce: a little oatmeal gives an unidentifiable extra quality to thatched cottage pie. She makes frequent and clever use of lovage, understands how to cook eel and pike, fish – from the Wye, in her case – which are not as regularly on English menus as they should be. Local perry appears with lamb and with pears. She draws, too, on the excellent cellar that they have built up. Curd cheese and milk are provided by their goats, eggs from the ornamental Peking bantams and chickens that peck in liberty around garden and courtyard. Thanks to

John Hegarty's planting, she has vegetables and fruit for the kitchen that may sound exotic or new, but were once part of the well-stocked 18th- and 19th-century English garden — cardoons, salsify, scorzonera, fennel, a variety of squashes and saladings and potatoes, mulberries, Spanish chestnuts, quinces and the right kinds of apple for a range of excellent puddings.

The natural ally of this style of food is the William Morris ideal of quality and good design in everyday things. The quiet interiors of Hope End, its particular peace, come from the beautiful wood of doors, window frames and floors, the tables and chairs from a Makepeace pupil, from the curtains of Welsh wool striped with natural dyes, the salad bowls from a turner at Hay on Wye. There is a sense of style running through the whole place from the grounds to the house itself, from the wine list to the menus.

Hope End turns its back on nothing that is good. It has a true sophistication, well-rooted, civilized, that is — at least in my experience — unique.

JANE GRIGSON

Contents

THE HISTORY OF HOPE END

Hope End has a romantic and chequered history. The name is derived from early English meaning 'House at the end of the hidden valley'. The first known dwelling was built in the 17th century, though there are traces of medieval stonework and more than a hint of iron age occupation on Oyster Hill nearby.

The house was soon enlarged, becoming the seat of Sir Henry Tempest in 1791. By this time two heiresses had already eloped from Hope End – the last, Sarah Lambert, to marry Sir Henry.

When Edward Moulton Barrett bought the estate he modified the existing house to become the stables of his exotic mansions which he built in Eastern style in 1809 to the designs of the Scottish landscape architect John Claudius Loudon. Few buildings in England were conceived in this idiom but the best known is Brighton Pavilion, also of the period. The grounds were laid out in the picturesque manner, but only traces remain.

Elizabeth Barrett Browning spent twenty-three happy years at Hope End, and frequent references are to be found in her poetry. She herself later eloped with Robert Browning from her home in Wimpole Street.

The Barretts were followed by the Heywood family, whose daughter Mary enjoyed an idyllic childhood at Hope End and later became another distinguished Victorian as wife of George Sumner, Bishop of Winchester, and founder of the Mothers' Union.

The Barrett mansion was demolished in 1873 – though the embellished stables and courtyards remain – and a fourth mansion was built on a site higher up the valley in more conventional Gothic style. This house was substantially gutted by fire in 1910 though a fragment survived, now restored as a much smaller house. That house, the grounds and stables deteriorated sadly from the fire until recent years when the estate was purchased by my family, who have lived in Herefordshire for many hundreds of years.

Clearance and renovation work continued at Hope End intermittently until 1975 when the stables and coach houses, by now a listed Grade 2 building, and the site of the first mansion, were restored and converted to their present use.

To Pomona
'Bountiful Goddess of Garden and Orchard
and all that grows therein.'

INTRODUCTION

There is a particular fascination in living and working in a place which has been inhabited for at least 700 years and probably a great deal longer. I am aware of treading in the same footsteps and performing the same rural tasks as so many have before me and it gives me a sense of perspective and timelessness which I find comforting.

I know that Roger and Juliana de Hope lived here in the 13th century but nothing more about them. I know that Sarah Skyppe of Ledbury married into the family here in the early part of the 18th century and brought with her her family's considerable horticultural skill and enthusiasm at a time which would have seen the building of the acre of walled garden, sitting snugly under the brow of the hill, tilted to the sun and protected by its ten foot high, rose and peach coloured brick walls. It was equipped with a hollow back wall heated by coal fires for the newly developed paraphernalia of graperies and peach houses and hot melon beds.

One hundred and fifty years ago Elizabeth Barrett Browning spent twenty three of her early years here and I can share with her, through vivid, intense and humorous writings, the same love of this place and its eccentric charm.

I have known and loved it for forty years though it has only been habitable again for fifteen. It has seen many changes of fortune, been subject to many vagaries and alterations and yet its essential character has remained intact.

It is this perspective which makes it easy for me to imagine the first horticultural activities here in medieval times, with the developing interest in herbs, the cultivation of vegetable and hedgerow plants and the increasing supplies of spices from the East. Then came the Tudor plantings. Gardeners were enthralled by fruit trees, a passion stimulated by writers like John Evelyn and culminating in the 18th-century surge of competence led by Richard Payne Knight – himself a resident of Herefordshire – and the extraordinary diverse plantings which would have taken place in the walled garden.

Salmon and pike were caught in the Wye; eels and game were taken from the ponds, hedgerows and woods of the estate; beef, lamb and pork, corn, milk and cheese came from the home farm at the gate, and cider and beer were brewed in the outbuildings of the house. All this, coupled with the intensive activity in the garden and the fashionable preoccupation with horticulture, makes this perhaps the great age of English gardening and eating.

I think this feeling of perspective enables me to look forward as easily and ask what food we will eat in the future.

There is now a renewed interest in gardening, but relatively little variety of food is grown in most gardens. There is an increasing demand for real food again but still so many eat processed or artificially grown food from abroad, flown in at all times of the year.

If you think that, in a season, an English garden can produce, to name only some, asparagus, seakale, artichokes, lettuce, carrot, beetroot, turnip, strawberry, raspberry, loganberry, black red and white currants, apple, pear, plum, and damson, quince, medlar, mulberry and peach, potato and parsnip, spinach, cabbage and cauliflower, a multitude of greens, peas and beans and an abundance of herbs, why are we always looking so covetously at the French? When you add to these delights English river and sea fish, unsurpassed beef and lamb when reared, killed and hung properly and some of the loveliest cheeses in the world, it is hard to believe that nearly everyone provides for himself from the supermarket.

So how should English food and cookery develop? Ideally straight back to the garden, and on to the smaller farm and smallholding where the interested amateur can grow such a variety of food for himself or where so many young people are trying to return to soundly based natural methods of agriculture and horticultural production for a living.

There are still small butchers who understand traditional methods of producing tasty tender meat and individual cheese makers who produce just enough for local demand. Food thus produced tastes better before you start to cook it as it has been subject to personal care and experience. All the cook has to do is seek out the best naturally produced ingredients in terms of freshness, ripeness and fullness of flavour and cook and present these simply and without fuss in a way which will enhance and not confuse the subtlety and delicacy of some dishes, the clear singing tastes of others.

English cooking has a wonderfully dense and complex heritage and tradition based on prime homegrown produce and centuries of trade with Europe, the East, the West Indies and the New World. Related to this is the undeniable inspiration of French cooking, brilliant techniques married to a passionate awareness and feeling for food, which inevitably influenced English cooks as history interwove the language and culture of the two countries. Unfortunately, this has sometimes led to a slavish adherence to and awe of French cuisine to the neglect of our own national dishes. A real revival of interest in English regional cookery will produce true regional variations instead of more French, Italian or Indian pastiches. Built on such promising foundations, the future of English cookery looks very exciting.

When my husband John and I decided to live at Hope End twenty years ago we realised that the place would have to earn its living because of the enormous cost of restoring the sadly neglected but madly romantic house and grounds. We decided to keep one wing ourselves and use the rest as a small hotel and restaurant.

My family has lived in Herefordshire for six hundred years and most of my recent ancestors have been involved with the land and food production in one way or another, as farmers, fruitgrowers, nurserymen, canners, vinegar brewers and so on. It was thus not difficult to decide to restore the acre of 18th-century walled garden to supply ourselves and our visitors with fruit, vegetables and herbs, particularly as John had been a keen participant in the organic movement for the previous ten years.

However, at that time all the hotels and restaurants around us for many miles with any pretensions of providing good food had French menus and boasted that their produce came from France or destinations further afield and even more exotic.

This struck us both as quite absurd and we decided it was time for the revolution. So we just started to cook English food with English ingredients. We had our own fruit, vegetables and herbs. We kept goats for delicious fresh, pure creamy milk which has provided a whole new approach to light cookery with curds and yogurt. Our orchard hens' lives have never been clouded by the shadow of a battery shed and they repay us with the quality of their eggs.

Our butcher in Ledbury selects his beef and lamb from local farms. Wye salmon, and pike and eels which no one seems to want much, from Hereford and the occasional Gloucester Old Spot ham completes the picture. A countryside groaning with the abundance of luscious goodies – what need have we of French produce!

With the exception of soft fruits, which we pick and freeze and serve as sauces and ice creams throughout the year, we enjoy the constraints of serving produce in season, hence the format of this book. It seems perverse to eat Californian strawberries in April when our better local and cheaper ones are available in abundance in June and July and the Autumn. The fullness of flavour and quality of fully ripe homegrown fruit can never be matched by the partially underripe specimens, grown for their hard skins, picked prematurely and packed and transported half way round the world.

A few of my recipes use ingredients which may be unfamiliar to some readers. Perry is a traditional English country drink similar to cider but made from pears. A few cider makers still produce it in Herefordshire.

The basic curd I use was familiar to Miss Muffet and her spider, and can be made as indicated on page 42. Some of the vegetables such as seakale, cardoon, butternut pumpkin and artichokes were well known to Victorian gardeners and gourmets and are as attractive to look at as they are to eat, as are the herbs which can be grown informally in flower beds or near to the kitchen door in little beds or tubs.

Quince and medlar trees are of a scale particularly suitable for small gardens. Morello cherries are very useful against northfacing walls; mulberries do not take as long to fruit as is made out; pears, apples, plums and damsons have much to recommend them as ornamental trees as well as bearing delicious fruits, so much more productive and harmonious than those boring and ubiquitous flowering cherries and cupressus. So at least some of these unusual ingredients are available to anyone with even a small garden, some foresight and an adaptive attitude.

I have tried to bring together these two strands: fresh English produce and a preference for a more relaxed approach to life. These are woven together in my recipes and the groups of menus for each season will, I hope, show the sort of balance which I believe will help all those who follow this way to a happy and healthy life with an English flavour.

I wrote the above ten years ago. Since then we have had scares over prime products such as eggs, cheese, milk, even carrots and now beef, unnerving for the consumers and traumatic for farmers. It would seem common sense that 'we are what we eat' and that this should apply to animals too. But common sense flies out of the window when cheaper food becomes the imperative. In an age obsessed with rights, sadly we need now to include the right of access to trustworthy, wholesome food.

There has also been intensification of the media's attention on cookery matched, paradoxically it seems, with a decline in home cooking. Of course it is easier to buy in a ready-made dish to put in the micro-wave after work, without the trouble of preparing and clearing up a meal, but I regret the demise of the satisfaction and creative fulfilment of planning, preparing and serving food in a close social context. On the other hand, perhaps now that food has become more of a hobby than a chore, there will be greater appreciation of the delights of beautiful ingredients and the sensuous experience of delicious food and readers may use some of their leisure time going out to eat food in a more discriminating and enjoyable way.

PATRICIA HEGARTY
Hope End, 1996

SPRING

Spring is the season of hope and promise and the rebirth of the year but it is also the season of shortage — the time of the hungry gap — when much of mankind in the northern hemisphere, until recently, suffered hunger and difficulty before the plenitude of the new season.

In relation to the production of food spring is the nadir; Lent is the time of fast to be followed by the renewal of hope in the rising on Easter Sunday. The symbol of Easter is the egg, the circle of eternity.

All this has faded from our minds with our technology and the ability to store and preserve food so that we are no longer aware of the elliptical nature of our food supplies, the sense of pattern and order in the progression of the seasons.

So, whilst the gardener is busy with his seeds and propagator in the comparative warmth of his greenhouse in March and April, he has not so much to bring to the kitchen door. The end of the stored potatoes and roots, some late-keeping apples like Sturmer Pippin or Brownlees Russet and if the weather is not too cruel the last of the leeks, broccoli, kale and cauliflower from the vegetable garden keep us going. Cook digs deeper into the freezer or in the preserving cupboard for soft fruits and plums, but the hens have started to lay well again with the lighter days, the goat kids and the cow calves.

Seakale and rhubarb are brought on under their terracotta forcing pots and the delicate shoots of some early herbs such as basil, chervil and summer savory make their appearance in the greenhouse. Outside, sorrel and chives begin to push through the earth and the crowns of lovage appear, poised to grow to over six feet high by June.

SORREL SOUP

After the long, bleak winter months spent eating the winter roots kept in earth clamps and cellars, the painstakingly salted meats and the dried stores, the first vivid green shoots of spring must have seemed almost miraculous to our forefathers. The tender young shoots of nettles, free for everyone to pick, were used for soup or as a vegetable, dandelion leaves for salads and in every cottage garden, the bright spears of sorrel, brought here by the Romans, were plucked for their delicious lemon-like sharpness.

SERVES: 6

PREPARATION TIME: minimal

COOKING TIME: 25 minutes

55g (2 oz) unsalted butter
1 small onion, chopped
1 small potato, peeled and thinly sliced
18 sorrel leaves
2 egg yolks, beaten (optional)
1.1 litres (2 pints) hot chicken stock *or* water
sea salt
freshly ground black pepper
garlic croûtons to garnish

1 Melt the butter in a large saucepan over a moderate heat and stir in the onion. Cook until softened, then add the potato to absorb the butter and continue cooking for a moment or two.

2 Wash the sorrel leaves, removing and discarding any thick red stems – they may be bitter. Tear the leaves into pieces and stir them around in the buttery mixture until the sorrel 'melts'. Add the stock or water, bring to the boil and simmer for 15 minutes. Remove from the heat and allow to cool slightly.

3 Purée the mixture in a blender and sieve back into the rinsed pan. Reheat gently, season with salt and pepper and serve. Garlic croûtons make a nice garnish.

This soup can be thickened and enriched by stirring in the beaten egg yolks just before serving, making sure the soup does not boil again. Beware of adding any cream – it may curdle!

This soup can also be made by adding the sorrel to the cooked ingredients just before puréeing the mixture, which makes the soup taste very green and raw. Personally, I prefer the more mellow taste of the longer-cooked sorrel.

MR BARRETT'S JAMAICAN SOUP

This is a marvellous deep green soup, lush, rich and comforting on cold Spring days. Use desiccated coconut if fresh sweet coconuts are hard to come by. However, fresh coconut really does add another dimension to the taste.

SERVES: 6

PREPARATION TIME: minimal

COOKING TIME: 25 minutes

55g (2 oz) unsalted butter
1 large onion, chopped
1.4 litres (2½ pints) hot chicken stock
55g (2 oz) long-grain brown rice, preferably Surinam
55g (2 oz) fresh grated coconut or desiccated coconut
sea salt
455g (1 lb) fresh spinach washed and trimmed of thick stems
freshly ground black pepper
3 tablespoonsful fresh double cream
freshly grated nutmeg
extra cream and grated nutmeg to garnish

1 Melt the butter in a large saucepan over a moderate heat and stir in the onion. Cook until the onion is transparent.

2 Pour the chicken stock in, increase the heat and, when it reaches boiling point, sprinkle in the rice and coconut. Simmer for 20 minutes.

3 Meanwhile, wash the spinach well and tear out the thickest stems and discard.

4 Press the leaves down in the hot stock and cook over a high heat for 5 minutes. Remove from the heat and allow to cool slightly.

5 Liquidize and sieve, pressing out every drop of liquid to extract the maximum flavour. Return to the rinsed out saucepan, season with salt and pepper, stir in the cream and grate in some nutmeg. Reheat gently and serve. A swirl of cream and a powdering of nutmeg make a pretty garnish.

CAULIFLOWER SOUP

In March and April, beautiful tight little cauliflowers come up from Cornwall, so fresh the leaves squeak as they are snapped away from the white curd. I like to use these green parts in this soup, which give it a delicate verdant tint.

SERVES: 6
PREPARATION TIME: 10 minutes
COOKING TIME: 25 minutes

1 small cauliflower
570ml (1 pint) chicken or ham stock
30g (1 oz) unsalted butter
30g (1 oz) wholemeal flour
570ml (1 pint) fresh milk
3 tablespoonsful fresh double cream
sea salt
freshly ground black pepper
paprika to garnish

1 Divide the cauliflower into tiny florets about the size of a small fingernail. Chop the bright-looking bits of stem and leaves and set aside.
2 Place the cauliflower florets in a medium-sized saucepan, add the chicken or ham stock, place over a moderate heat and simmer for 5 minutes. Remove the florets with a slotted spoon and set aside. Add the reserved stems and leaves to the remaining stock and cook until soft, about 5–10 minutes. Remove from the heat and allow to cool slightly.
3 Liquidize, then sieve and reserve.
4 Melt the butter over a moderate heat in the rinsed out saucepan. Stir in the flour and cook for 1 minute. Gradually add the puréed cauliflower mixture and the milk, bring to the boil and cook for 4–5 minutes to thicken slightly. Add the cream and the reserved florets and season with salt and pepper. Decorate the soup with a pinch of paprika sprinkled over each bowl and serve with chunks of crusty wholemeal bread and butter.

ASPARAGUS

It is always a thrill to see the first spears of asparagus pushing through the ground in April — it marks a certain point in the year.

Asparagus is at its best simply tied in bundles and set upright in boiling water with the heads sticking out (covered with an aluminium foil 'hat' so that they are cooked by the steam). A proper asparagus steamer does make this easier. The cooking time depends on the age and thickness of the spears — anything from 5–15 minutes. Test the stems with a fork. The tender flower heads of the asparagus will collapse and spoil if overcooked, so err if anything on the other side.

Any asparagus which is not top-quality, or maybe the spindly sprue of the first year's undeveloped growth, may be made into a sumptuous soup, used as a filling for little tartlets, eked out with pieces of chicken or salmon, or enjoyed as a filling for these appetizing little pancakes.

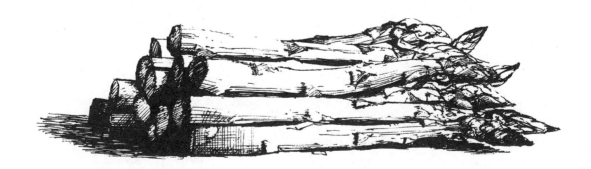

ASPARAGUS PANCAKES

SERVES: 6
PREPARATION TIME: 10 minutes
COOKING TIME: 20–25 minutes

PANCAKE BATTER	FILLING
2 free range eggs	approximately 24 asparagus spears
115g (4 oz) wholemeal flour	sea salt
285ml (½ pint) fresh milk	freshly ground black pepper
1 tablespoon gin	55g (2 oz) unsalted butter, plus extra butter
sea salt	for greasing
30g (1 oz) unsalted butter for frying	beurre manié (optional)
	1 tablespoonful fresh finely-grated Parmesan cheese
	120ml (4 fl oz) soured cream

1 First make the batter. Place all the ingredients except the butter in a blender and blend for 1 minute on the fastest speed. If you are not planning to cook the pancakes immediately, leave the batter in the blender jug and set aside in a cool place. Whizz again briefly before proceeding.

2 Put a little knob of butter in a small frying pan, about 12.5cm (5 inches) in diameter, and melt it over a moderate heat until the butter just begins to smoke. Tip in just enough batter to cover the base of the pan. Cook until lightly set and then turn over with a spatula or fish slice or toss if you are feeling brave. Cook each pancake for about 30 seconds on the reverse side. You should be able to make 12 very light, thin, lacy little pancakes. The small amount of gin helps keep these wholemeal pancakes light – rather than adding a flavour of its own to the batter.

3 Make the filling. Cook the asparagus, cut off the choice top 7cm (3 inches) and set aside. Discard any of the stalk that is obviously hard and woody and purée the remainder. Push through a sieve to obtain a light green sauce. Season lightly and stir in the butter while the sauce is still warm. If it seems too watery, stabilize it with a little beurre manié.

4 Preheat the oven to 450°F/230°C/Gas mark 8, or heat the grill to medium. Grease a baking sheet generously with butter.

5 Lay 4 asparagus tips down the centre of each pancake, moisten with some of the asparagus sauce and roll up the pancakes, making sure that the asparagus tips peep out of the ends. Stripe the pancakes with soured cream and dust with Parmesan cheese. Place the pancake rolls on the baking sheet and bake in the oven for about 8 minutes, or place under the grill if you like your pancakes crispy at the edges.

SALMON

The finest salmon run up our rivers in the cold, blustery days of March and April. These wild salmon are full of vigour. Their flesh is firm and their flavour cannot be compared with their flabbier, less lustrous, pellet-fed cousins from the salmon farm.

Don't spoil this royal fish with exotic ingredients. Wild salmon is sufficiently rich and flavoured to stand on its own. Simply bake a steak in buttered aluminium foil with a bay leaf, moistened with a little white wine or dry cider and serve with a lemon butter, parsley or tarragon sauce. There is usually some fresh tarragon in the cold greenhouse by now.

A good way to use the tail of a salmon is in these tartlets. If you wish to serve this as a main course, the pastry can be baked in a 22.5cm (9-inch) fluted flan tin. However, individual brioche tins make particularly ornamental individual containers for a starter.

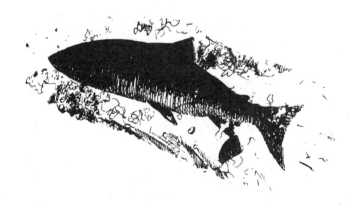

SALMON TAIL TARTLETS

SERVES: 6 as a starter *or* 4 as a main course
PREPARATION TIME: Making the pastry,
plus 15 minutes
BAKING TIME: 15 minutes
COOKING TIME: 20–25 minutes

I recipe quantity wholemeal shortcrust pastry (page 176)

FILLING

155g (1 lb) lightly cooked salmon tail, reserving the skin and bones	2 teaspoonsful made up English mustard
	juice of ½ lemon
140ml (¼ pint) salmon stock, made from the skin and bones of the salmon	2 tablespoonsful grated farmhouse Cheddar cheese
tail, plus cider, white wine or water (see below)	1 tablespoonful chopped fresh tarragon
	sea salt
30g (1 oz) unsalted butter	freshly ground black pepper
30g (1 oz) wholemeal flour	wholemeal breadcrumbs
140ml (¼ pint) fresh single cream or milk	fresh English parsley to garnish

1 Make the pastry and let it rest for at least 20 minutes.

2 Preheat the oven to 400°F/200°C/Gas mark 6.

3 Divide the pastry into 6 portions and roll out into thin circles. Line 6 greased brioche tins (or 1 x 22.6cm (9 inch) flan tin).

4 Bake blind for 10 minutes following the directions on page 176.

5 Make the filling. Detach the skin and bones from the salmon and place in a medium-sized saucepan. Cover with cider, white wine or water and bring very slowly to the boil. Remove from the heat, allow the stock to cool, then strain.

6 Prepare the sauce with the remaining ingredients, except for the breadcrumbs and parsley, stirring it vigorously until it thickens.

7 Break up the salmon into large flakes and gently stir into the sauce. Fill the pastry cases (still supported by the brioche tins) and scatter over the breadcrumbs.

8 Heat through under a moderate grill for 8–10 minutes. To extract the tartlets from the tins, I hold the hot tins with kitchen tongs and ease the pastry out with a curved grapefruit knife. Serve immediately, garnished with a tuft of English parsley.

POTATOES

Potatoes are high on our list of favourite vegetables. We wait in anticipation for the first of our early potatoes to be lifted — long after the flood of little new potatoes from Egypt and Cyprus — and keep on using our main crop to the last sack, because they taste and cook so much better than any you can buy. Organically grown potatoes have a strong, earthy taste and vitality so lacking in the chemically fertilized ones. The use of nitrates encourages larger tubers, but they are very inferior in flavour. When you spear them with a skewer, a spray of water shoots out, diluting the taste and weakening the texture.

GARLIC POTATOES

SERVES: 6
PREPARATION TIME: 15 minutes
BAKING TIME: 1½ hours

680g (1½ lb) potatoes
6 cloves garlic, finely chopped
sea salt
freshly ground black pepper
180ml (6 fl oz) fresh single cream

1 Preheat the oven to 350°F/180°C/Gas mark 4.
2 Peel the potatoes and slice very thinly. In an ovenproof dish, alternate layers of potato, garlic and seasoning. Pour over the cream.
3 Bake for approximately 1½ hours, until the potatoes are tender. Serve immediately, or the potatoes will dry out.

GREEN GARLIC POTATOES

This is a family recipe, given to me by a friend. It is a delicious way of using the attractive white-flowered wild garlic, which grows so profusely in shady places in the Spring. You could use chopped chives instead of the garlic leaves, but the result will just not be the same.

SERVES: 6
PREPARATION TIME: 10 minutes
COOKING TIME: approximately 20 minutes

680g (1½ lb) potatoes
60g (2 oz) unsalted butter
sea salt
freshly ground black pepper
fresh wild garlic leaves

1 Peel, cook and mash the potatoes with the butter and seasoning as in Riced Potatoes (page 25).
2 Tear the garlic leaves into small pieces – you will have to experiment to see how many you need – and stir into the mashed potatoes. Serve piping hot.

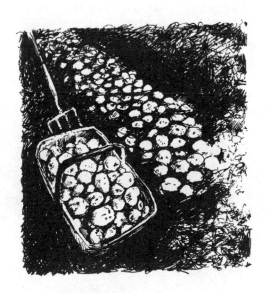

PAN HAGGERTY

There is no need for me to justify including this recipe from the North. Slivers of potato are fried in beef dripping with stratas of onion and cheese to make a hearty country dish that will stick to the ribs and keep the cold out.

SERVES: 6

PREPARATION TIME: 30 minutes

COOKING TIME: 30–40 minutes per batch

900g (2 lb) main crop potatoes
2 medium-sized onions
115g (4 oz) farmhouse Cheddar or Llanboidy cheese
85g (3 oz) beef dripping
sea salt
freshly ground black pepper

1 Peel the potatoes and grate them into flakes. Rinse in cold water to remove excess starch and dry on a clean tea towel. Slice the onions thinly and grate the cheese. Unless you have an enormous frying pan (or two large ones), it is best to cook this amount in two batches.
2 Melt 30g (1 oz) of the dripping in a large, heavy frying pan over moderate heat. Layer one-quarter of the potatoes, half the onions and seasoning and another quarter of potatoes in the pan. Cook until well browned on the bottom, about 15–20 minutes, turn over using a large fish slice, add 15g (½ oz) more dripping and cook on the other side for about 15–20 minutes. When the second side is browned, turn out onto a heated serving plate and keep warm while you cook the second batch. Serve immediately.

RICED POTATOES

A very light, airy way with potatoes.

SERVES: 6
PREPARATION TIME: 20 minutes
COOKING TIME: approximately 20 minutes,
depending on size
BAKING TIME: 20 minutes

680g (1½ lb) floury potatoes
55g (2 oz) unsalted butter
sea salt
freshly ground black pepper
freshly grated nutmeg

1 Peel the potatoes and cook in boiling water until tender. Drain and mash with butter and seasonings.

2 While the potatoes are still warm, squeeze through a potato ricer (see below) into an ovenproof dish. On no account should you try to rearrange the fine filaments with a fork or the appearance will be spoilt.

3 Half an hour before serving, preheat the oven to 400°F/200°C/Gas mark 6. Bake the potatoes until the top strands have caught and browned, about 20 minutes. This dish will also keep very well in a warm oven.

The best way to obtain the correct texture for this dish is with a potato ricer, which is sold in kitchen shops, sometimes under the name *kartoffelpresse*. This implement can also be used to purée chestnuts.

HAUT-BAKED POTATOES

The curd cheese can be omitted from this recipe, but it does have a remarkable bouffant effect. A variety of herbs can be used and toasted sesame seeds or poppy seeds may be substituted for the celery seed. I make my own curd cheese from goat's milk. See the recipe on page 42.

SERVES: 6

PREPARATION TIME: 10–15 minutes

BAKING TIME: 1¼–1½ hours

6 medium-sized main crop potatoes
115g (4 oz) unsalted butter
3 tablespoonsful rolled organic porridge oats
2 free-range eggs, beaten
115g (4 oz) curd cheese (optional)
sea salt
freshly ground black pepper
1 teaspoonful celery seeds and/or chopped fresh sweet
marjoram, chives, parsley, fennel, celery leaves or any other
seasonal herbs and/or toasted sesame seeds or poppy seeds
55g (2 oz) grated farmhouse Cheddar cheese
paprika

1 Preheat the oven to 400°F/200°C/Gas mark 6.

2 Scrub the potatoes, push a metal skewer through each one and bake for 45 minutes–1 hour, depending on the size of the potatoes. When they are done, remove from the oven, but leave the oven on.

3 Cut the potatoes in half lengthways, scoop out the flesh and mash up with all the remaining ingredients, except for the Cheddar cheese and paprika. Pile the mixture back into the potato skins and scatter with the cheese and paprika.

4 Bake for 30 minutes. If the tops are not already brown, finish off under the grill. Serve piping hot.

GRATIN POTATOES

This dish is slightly less rich than the recipe for garlic potatoes and is easier to time correctly. It must be served immediately after baking or the potatoes will dry out.

SERVES: 6
PREPARATION TIME: 15 minutes
COOKING TIME: approximately 20 minutes
BAKING TIME: 15 minutes

680g (1 1/2 lb) potatoes

WHITE SAUCE

30g (1 oz) unsalted butter
30g (1 oz) wholemeal flour
120ml (4 fl oz) fresh milk
120ml (4 fl oz) fresh single cream
sea salt
freshly ground black pepper

1 Peel the potatoes and cook in boiling salt water until tender. Drain, allow to cool, then slice into rounds. Arrange in an ovenproof dish.
2 Meanwhile, make the white sauce using the above ingredients. Pour evenly over the potatoes.
3 Approximately 30 minutes before serving, preheat the oven to 450°F/230°C/Gas mark 8. Bake the potatoes for 15 minutes.

SOUFFLÉ POTATOES

This is a rather rich way of serving potatoes, but it is redeemed by its light texture.

SERVES: 6
PREPARATION TIME: 10 minutes
COOKING TIME: approximately 20 minutes
BAKING TIME: 40 minutes

680g (1 ½ lb) potatoes
60g (2 oz) unsalted butter
sea salt
freshly ground black pepper
2 free-range eggs, separated
55g (2 oz) curd cheese (see page 42)

1 Peel, cook and mash the potatoes with the butter and seasoning as in Riced Potatoes (page 25). Mix in the egg yolks.
2 Fluff up the curd cheese lightly with a fork and mix gently into the potatoes.
3 Preheat the oven to 400°F/200°C/Gas mark 6.
4 Whisk the egg whites until stiff, but not dry and fold gently, but thoroughly into the mixture. Pile into an ovenproof dish and bake for about 40 minutes. The potatoes should puff up, with a lovely gilded crust. Serve immediately.

CARROT AND APPLE SALAD

A favourite and familiar salad

SERVES: 6
PREPARATION TIME: minimal

	DRESSING
3 medium-sized carrots	3 tablespoonsful walnut oil
3 strongly-flavoured dessert apples, such	1–1½ teaspoonful cider vinegar
as Kings Acre Pippin	sea salt
55g (2 oz) raisins	
90ml (3 fl oz) fresh orange juice	
55g (2 oz) walnuts	
30g (1 oz) sunflower seeds	
few sprigs fresh English parsley	
fresh mint leaves, if available	

1 Wash the carrots and apples and grate into a bowl, leaving the skins on if possible.
2 Soak the raisins in the orange juice and add to the carrot and apple mixture.
3 Mix in the walnuts, sunflower seeds, parsley and mint, tearing the parsley and mint leaves rather than chopping them.
4 Mix the dressing ingredients together and toss with the salad a little before serving as this salad gains by being dressed slightly in advance.

CARROTS WITH MUSTARD SAUCE

This jaunty display of orange and gold is a marvellous pick-me-up for ageing carrots. It is a good accompaniment for grilled meats, such as the Lamb Noisettes in Rosemary and Perry Sauce on page 34.

Try to use lemon thyme if you can, it is so refreshing. Mint would be a good alternative.

SERVES: 6
PREPARATION TIME: 15 minutes
COOKING TIME: 15–20 minutes

680g (1½ lb) old carrots
30g (1 oz) unsalted butter

MUSTARD SAUCE

2 egg yolks	unrefined light muscovado sugar
1 clove garlic, chopped	sea salt
2 tablespoonsful cider vinegar	freshly ground black pepper
140ml (¼ pint) cold pressed olive oil	1 tablespoon lightly chopped fresh lemon thyme
juice of ½ lemon	or mint leaves
1 tablespoonful made up English mustard	lemon thyme or mint leaves to garnish

1 Peel the carrots and either cut into 5 x .5cm (2 x ¼-inch) sticks or rounds. Cook until almost tender, then add the butter at the finishing stage, allowing any excess water to evaporate. Remove from the heat, transfer to a serving bowl and keep warm.

2 Put the egg yolks and garlic in a blender or food processor and start whizzing. Add the vinegar and then the oil, pouring it slowly and carefully down the spout until the sauce thickens. Briefly whizz in the lemon juice, some of the mustard, a little sugar and seasoning. If the sauce is too thick, mix in a little cold water, one teaspoonful at a time. Taste and add more lemon juice, mustard, sugar and seasoning according to your preference. Stir in the lemon thyme or mint.

3 Warm the sauce in a basin over hot water, stirring frequently. To serve, blanket the carrots with mustard sauce and garnish with sprigs of lemon thyme.

SEAKALE WRAPPED IN HAM

Seakale, an exquisitely attractive plant of the pebbled foreshore, which grows in the inland garden easily, needs to be blanched under terracotta pots for a few weeks before pulling.

This vegetable is deliciously crisp eaten raw in a salad and can also be cooked. Toss the washed and trimmed stalks into a little boiling water for 5–10 minutes or steam for about 15 minutes – testing to see when they are just tender enough to bite through. Serve with melted butter and lemon juice, salt and pepper and possibly a light dusting of finely grated Cheddar.

For this recipe it is worthwhile tracking down a really nice farmhouse ham though this may be difficult.

SERVES: 6

PREPARATION TIME: 20 minutes

COOKING TIME: 15–20 minutes

6 thin slices of traditionally-reared ham
18–24 seakale stalks, plus some leaves for garnish

MUSTARD MAYONNAISE

2 egg yolks	1–2 teaspoonsful English mustard
3 tablespoonsful cider vinegar, or to taste	made up with single cream
285ml (½ pint) cold pressed olive oil	freshly ground black pepper
sea salt	chopped fresh English parsley
	fresh seakale leaves to garnish

1 Cut the colourful, frilly leaves off the seakale and reserve for garnish. Wash the stalks to remove any earth and cook in boiling water for about 15 minutes, depending on their thickness. When tender, drain and set aside.

2 Thirty minutes before making the mayonnaise, bring the ingredients up to room temperature.

3 Make the mayonnaise. Put the egg yolks and half the vinegar in a blender or food processor. Whizz for a moment, then add the oil in a thin stream down the spout, until the mayonnaise thickens and has absorbed all the oil. Add more vinegar to taste as you go and if the mixture is too thick, dilute it carefully with a little water to the consistency of thick cream. Add as much mustard and seasoning as you think suitable.

4 Spread a little mayonnaise over each slice of ham, sprinkle with parsley, lay 3–4 stalks of seakale on top and roll up. Serve garnished with fresh seakale leaves and hand round a bowl of mustard mayonnaise.

PIKE WITH WATERCRESS SAUCE

The dense white meat of the pike is a treat. It is delicious served in fillets, hot or cold, or made up into Pike Dumplings with Dill and Tomato Sauce (page 158).

SERVES: 6 as a main course
PREPARATION TIME: 20 minutes
BAKING TIME: 45 minutes
COOKING TIME: 15 minutes

I whole pike, about 2.3kg (5 lb)
570ml (I pint) white wine or dry cider
I bay leaf
½ medium-sized onion
6 black peppercorns

WATERCRESS SAUCE

6 shallots, finely chopped
6 tablespoons cider vinegar or wine vinegar
285ml (½ pint) fish stock (from the cooking liquor)
225g (9 oz) unsalted butter
3 bunches watercress
sea salt
freshly ground black pepper

1 Preheat the oven to 375°F/190°C/Gas mark 5.

2 Chop the head and tail off the pike. Wrap the fish in a foil parcel moistened with the wine or cider, place the parcel in a roasting tin and bake for approximately 45 minutes or until cooked. Remove from the oven and allow to cool.

3 Remove the thick skin, which will now peel off cleanly. It should now be easy to divide the fish into fillets, extracting the bones at the same time.

4 Pour the cooking liquor into a saucepan, add the bay leaf, onion and peppercorns and reduce, over a high heat, to 285ml (½ pint). Strain into a clean jug and reserve.

5 Place the shallots, vinegar and 30g (1 oz) of the butter in the rinsed out saucepan and reduce to 1 tablespoonful. Remove from the heat.

6 Add the reserved fish stock and whizz in a blender with half the watercress, which you have broken into pieces.

7 Place the watercress mixture in a saucepan over a very gentle heat and whisk in the

remaining butter piece by piece until the sauce thickens and is glossy and smooth. Just before serving, reserve 6 whole sprigs of watercress for garnish, shred the remaining watercress and add to the sauce at the last moment. (This will ensure that it retains its bright colour.) Season with salt and pepper to taste.

8 Warm the pike fillets between two dinner plates over a steaming pan of water. Watch carefully as you do not want to cook the fish any further.

9 Serve the fish neatly surrounded by a pool of sauce, highlighted by the watercress leaves.

My great grandmother Maria included a short recipe, 'Gravy for a Pike' in her cookery notebook.

'Stew a piece of coarse beef in 1 pint water, with a few peppercorns and an onion till it has wasted nearly half, then strain it off and add a little soy and ketchup, a little flour and butter to thicken it.' It seems a strange combination of meat and fish, although anchovies were often used to spice up beef. She must have thought that pike merited strong treatment!

PHOTOGRAPHS:

Sorrel soup; Herefordshire Beef Olives in Cider Sauce; Carrots with Mustard Sauce
Salmon Tail Tartlets; Seakale wrapped in Ham
Rhubarb and Honey Jelly

LAMB NOISETTES IN
ROSEMARY AND PERRY SAUCE

There is a lot of fat on lamb so, with modern tastes in mind, I pare down cutlets to a small nugget of meat, wrapped round with a fine band of crisped skin. As a lot of the essential flavour is contained in the fat and the bones, I use some of this to make the sauce.

SERVES: 6
PREPARATION TIME: 20 minutes
ROASTING TIME: 45 minutes
COOKING TIME: 40 minutes
GRILLING TIME: 12 minutes

12–18 lamb cutlets, depending on size
1 small onion, chopped
1 small carrot, chopped
1 celery stalk, sliced
1 bay leaf
fresh English parsley
30g (1 oz) wholemeal flour
285ml (½ pint) perry
lamb stock (see below)
1 teaspoonful tamari
sea salt
freshly ground black pepper
fresh rosemary sprigs
medlar or redcurrant jelly to serve

1 Bone the lamb cutlets. Remove the eye of the meat and carefully pare away most of the fat along the length of the cutlet until you are left with a thin strip of skin. Wrap this round the eye of the meat and secure with a cocktail stick.
2 Preheat the oven to 400°F/200°C/Gas mark 6. Put the bones, some of the fat scraps, onion, carrot and celery in a roasting tin and bake, turning from time to time until the bones and vegetables are browned, about 45 minutes. Remove from the oven and strain off the fat. Reserve both fat and vegetables and cool.
3 Make the stock. Put the cooked bones and vegetables in a saucepan with the bay leaf and parsley and cover with water. Bring to the boil, reduce the heat and simmer for 30 minutes.

Strain the stock into a jug.

4 Make the sauce. Melt 30g (1 oz) of the reserved lamb fat in a saucepan, add the flour and cook for 1 minute. Stir in the perry vigorously and add the tamari and any meat jelly which has collected beneath the remaining set fat and a sprig of rosemary. Make up the sauce to the desired consistency with the lamb stock. Cook for about 5 minutes, whisking to keep the sauce smooth.

5 Heat the grill to medium high. Grill the lamb noisettes for about 12 minutes turning them three times. When done, transfer the lamb to a serving dish and keep warm. Remove the cocktail sticks, mix any meat juices from the grill pan into the sauce and strain through a fine sieve into a warm gravy boat or jug and serve each portion garnished with a sprig of rosemary and a spoonful of medlar or redcurrant jelly.

If you prefer a lighter sauce, omit the lamb fat and flour and add 1 teaspoonful cornflour to the perry and meat jelly.

HEREFORDSHIRE BEEF OLIVES
IN CIDER SAUCE

The term 'olive' refers to the shape of these little meat rolls. The *Oxford English Dictionary* records the first use of this word as a cooking term in 1588. The rich pastures of Herefordshire raise prime beef and I have found references to beef and veal olives in old local recipe books.

SERVES: 6
PREPARATION TIME: 30 minutes
COOKING TIME: 30 minutes
BAKING TIME: 1 hour

900g (2 lb) well-hung topside of beef
225g (½ lb) unsmoked bacon, thinly sliced

STUFFING	CIDER SAUCE
55g (2 oz) wholemeal breadcrumbs	225g (½ lb) ripe tomatoes
1 medium-sized onion, finely chopped	3 tablespoonsful cold pressed olive oil
1 teaspoonful finely chopped fresh thyme	570ml (1 pint) dry cider
rind and juice of ½ lemon	beef stock or water
1 egg yolk	2 level teaspoonsful cornflour
2 tablespoonsful tomato purée	sea salt
sea salt	freshly ground black pepper
freshly ground black pepper	chopped fresh English parsley to garnish

1 Cut as many thin slices – about 5 x 10cm (2 x 4 inches) – as possible from the beef joint. Blanch the bacon for 2 minutes in boiling water and cut off the rinds. Gently soften the tomatoes in a saucepan over a moderate heat (adding a little water will prevent them from burning). Remove from the heat and sieve thoroughly.

2 Combine the stuffing ingredients into a thick, crumbly paste.

3 Snip the bacon into small strips and lay one strip along each slice of beef. Spread a portion of stuffing on top, roll up and secure with a cocktail stick.

4 Preheat the oven to 300°F/150°C/Gas mark 2. Heat the oil in a frying pan and brown the beef olives in batches, transferring them to a casserole when done. When all the beef olives are browned, add the sieved tomato, cider and enough beef stock or water to the casserole to cover the meat. Bake for 1 hour, or until the beef is tender.

5 Transfer the beef olives from the casserole to a covered serving dish and keep warm.

Remove the cocktail sticks. Reduce the cooking juices to 425ml (¾ pint). Strain the reduced liquid and thicken with the cornflour. Add salt and pepper to taste.

6 To serve, arrange the beef olives side by side and spoon some sauce over. Dot with chopped parsley to bring up the colour of the sauce.

WILD WOOD PIGEON
WITH LOVAGE

Herefordshire is renowned for the number and charming variety of its dovecotes. Pigeons used to be a valuable source of nutrition during the long winter months and in the often inclement Spring that followed. In this recipe the perry and lovage ameliorate too 'high' a flavour.

SERVES: 6
PREPARATION TIME: 10 minutes
BAKING TIME: 2½–3 hours (see note below)
COOKING TIME: 10 minutes

2 tablespoonsful sunflower oil
6 plump wild wood pigeons
1 medium-sized onion, chopped
few fresh lovage leaves
1.7 litres (3 pints) dry perry
1 tablespoonful cornflour
1 tablespoonful tamari
sea salt
freshly ground black pepper

1 Preheat the oven 300°F/150°C/Gas mark 2. Heat the oil in a capacious frying pan and brown the breasts of the pigeons. Remove from the heat and fit them 'head down' in a casserole. Sprinkle with the onions, tuck in the lovage leaves and cover with perry.
2 Cook the pigeon casserole in the oven for 2½–3 hours, until the breasts are tender. Strain off most of the juice and keep warm while you prepare the sauce.
3 Strain the remaining cooking juice into a saucepan and reduce over a high heat to approximately 425ml (¾ pint). Taste and add a few more lovage leaves if necessary. Thicken the sauce slightly with the cornflour. Strain through a fine sieve and season with the tamari and salt and pepper.
4 Cut the breasts off the pigeons and return to the warm liquid. Keep the remaining parts of the bird to make stock for game soup.
5 To serve, quickly drain each pigeon breast on a piece of absorbent kitchen paper and arrange on a warmed serving plate, surrounded by a sauce set off with glossy green lovage leaves.

Note: Birds reared for the table suit modern palates and will need less cooking time than I have allowed for my wild wood pigeons of indeterminate age.

Use the lovage sparingly; it is a powerful herb, especially in the early vigorous growing months of the year.

RHUBARB AND HONEY JELLY

This is a very light and pretty coral-pink jelly — the sharpness of the rhubarb counteracted by honeyed sweetness. Select and pull only the brightest red young rhubarb stalks. The tenderest and pinkest come early from the forcing pots. I find leaf gelatine much easier to use than the powdered sort and it has no hint of taste.

SERVES: 6
PREPARATION TIME: 15 minutes
COOKING TIME: 30–35 minutes
CHILLING TIME: 4 hours

900g (2 lb) fresh rhubarb
2 tablespoonsful water
3 tablespoonsful honey, or to taste
6 leaves gelatine
fresh whipped cream and toasted almonds to serve

1 Cut the rhubarb into 2.5cm (1-inch) lengths, discarding the white or green parts of the stalk.

2 Put the rhubarb in a heavy saucepan with the water and cook until very soft and juicy, about 30 minutes. Strain off the juice into a measuring jug — you will need 850ml (1½ pints). If there is a shortfall, put that amount of water in the pan with the rhubarb pulp and cook for a further 5 minutes. Strain this liquid into the jug containing the rhubarb juice and dissolve the honey in the liquid while it is still warm.

3 Meanwhile, cover the leaf gelatine with a little cold water and leave to soak in a shallow dish.

4 When the rhubarb juice has cooled to blood heat, carefully stir in the soaked gelatine pieces one by one. Make sure no lumps of gelatine remain, strain the mixture once more and pour into a glass bowl or individual wine glasses. Chill in the refrigerator. The jellies should be firm within 4 hours.

5 To serve, decorate with whipped cream and toasted almond flakes.

GOOSEBERRY AND ELDERFLOWER CREAM

Gooseberries are special as one of the first fruits of the year, traditionally making their first appearance at Whitsun, married with the delicate white lace and haunting perfume of elderflowers. The word 'cream' in the recipe is misleading, since no cream is involved. Egg yolks and a little butter are used to produce a smooth purée the consistency and richness of cream. When elderflowers are not available, orange flower water makes a very appealing substitute.

SERVES: 6

PREPARATION TIME: minimal

COOKING TIME: 20–30 minutes

900g (2 lb) fresh gooseberries
1 elderflower head or 1 tablespoonful orange flower water
115g (4 oz) unrefined golden granulated sugar, or to taste
3 egg yolks
115g (4 oz) unsalted butter
tiny elderflowers to garnish
thick fresh Jersey cream and thin almond biscuits to serve

1 Tip the gooseberries into a saucepan with the elderflower and 2 tablespoonsful water and cook over a very low heat until they soften, about 20–30 minutes. If orange flower water is used, add to the purée after the butter. Remove the elderflower and rub the gooseberries through a sieve very thoroughly. Discard the seeds and skins and sweeten the gooseberry purée with the sugar.

2 Return the gooseberry purée to the saucepan over a very low heat and beat in the egg yolks and the butter, bit by bit. When the purée is nice and thick, cool or chill until ready to serve. Garnish the light green 'cream' with thick, yellow Jersey cream and some tiny, lacy elderflowers. Serve with almond biscuits.

CURDS AND WHEY

Curd is an exceptionally traditional and versatile foodstuff and can be used in sweet or savoury dishes or on its own, taking colour and life from the addition of herbs and spices, or incorporated with eggs, vegetables, fruits or nuts, or used as a stuffing for fish or chicken. Cheesecake, which we think of as an American invention, was, in fact, taken to America by the Pilgrim fathers. Whey, the sweet liquid that drips from the curd, can be substituted for other liquids in breads and soups.

HOME-MADE CURD CHEESE

MAKES: approximately 115g (4 oz) curd cheese, plus 2.3 litres (3½ pints) whey
COOKING TIME: 10 minutes
DRIPPING TIME: overnight

2.3 litres (4 pints) fresh milk (goat's for preference)
2 tablespoonsful cider vinegar or lemon juice

1 Heat the milk in a large, deep saucepan just to the boiling point. Lift off the heat and stir in the vinegar or lemon juice. The milk should separate into curds and whey. If it does not, add a little more vinegar, very carefully, in small amounts. Too much, and the curd cheese will be hard and rubbery.
2 Strain through a muslin cloth and hang up over a basin to drip in a cool place. Use within 24 hours.

If you are using shop-bought curd for any of the recipes in this book, make sure it is drained of excess moisture as above.

APRICOT CURD TART

This is a useful pudding for the Spring as it uses dried apricots from the store cupboard – in a season when really ripe, fresh fruit is still at a premium – combined with curd made from an ever-increasing daily milk supply. The recipe lends itself to endless adaptations but is best with intensely-flavoured fruits such as blackcurrants and damsons.

MAKES: 1 x 22.5cm (9-inch) tart
SOAKING TIME: overnight (optional)
PREPARATION TIME: 10 minutes
BAKING TIME: 10–15 minutes
COOKING TIME: 20 minutes

OATMEAL AND HONEY BASE

85g (3 oz) rolled organic porridge oats

85g (3 oz) unsalted butter

45g (1½ oz) unrefined light muscovado sugar

45g (1½ oz) honey

FILLING

340g (¾ lb) dried apricots pieces

115g (4 oz) whole dried apricots

425ml (¾ pint) fresh apple juice

lemon juice (optional)

2 tablespoonsful fresh single cream

2 tablespoonsful finely ground unrefined
demerara sugar

few drops natural vanilla essence

340g (¾ lb) curd cheese (see page 42)

apricot jam or apple jelly to glaze

fresh double cream to serve

1 First make the base. In a medium-sized saucepan, melt all the ingredients together over a low heat. Remove from the heat and mix well to amalgamate.
2 Preheat the oven to 400°F/200°C/Gas mark 6. Turn the oat mixture into a fluted 22.5cm (9-inch) flan tin with a removable base. Spread the mixture evenly over the base of the tin and bake for about 10–15 minutes, until firm and lightly browned. Set aside to cool.
3 Make the filling. Soften the apricot pieces and whole apricots separately by simmering them slowly in the apple juice. (The whole apricots may respond to simply soaking overnight.) Process the apricot pieces to a purée, adding lemon juice if it seems appropriate.
4 Pour the cream into a cup with the vanilla essence and dissolve the sugar in it. Turn the curd into a bowl and lightly fold in the cream mixture. Spread the curd over the base in the tin, pressing it into the fluting. Cover with the apricot purée and set the whole apricots into this. Glaze the tart with a little warmed apricot jam or apple jelly.
5 When the outer ring of the flan tin is removed, the curd should mould to a firm fluted pattern which is quite striking.
6 Serve with extra cream.

CHOCOLATE CHEESECAKE

Select the best bitter chocolate you can for this wonderfully textured and wickedly seductive pudding.

SERVES: 8–10
SOAKING TIME: 1 hour
PREPARATION TIME: 30 minutes
CHILLING TIME: 2–3 days

115g (4 oz) raisins
4 tablespoons Calvados
2 leaves gelatine
3 tablespoonsful strong brewed coffee
340g (¾ lb) bitter chocolate
55g (2 oz) unsalted butter
455g (1 lb) curd cheese (see page 42)
6 egg yolks, beaten
8 egg whites
grated chocolate or small Spring flowers to decorate

1 Soak the raisins in the Calvados for 1 hour.
2 Soak the gelatine in a dish of cold water for 5–10 minutes. Dissolve completely in the warmed coffee.
3 Melt the chocolate in a bowl over hot water. Cream the butter and cheese together in a food processor. When the chocolate is melted, remove from the heat and add the egg yolks and raisin and Calvados mixture. Combine well with the butter and curd. Stir in the gelatine and coffee liquid very thoroughly.
4 Whisk the egg whites until stiff, but not dry and carefully fold into the curd mixture. Turn out into a 23cm (9-inch) spring clip cake tin, which has been lined with clingfilm. Cover with foil and refrigerate for 2–3 days before eating.
5 Unmould the cake. Decorate with grated chocolate or small Spring flowers such as violets for a brighter effect.

Yogurt

Yogurt has only been widely known in this country since the last war, but has rapidly been established as an important ingredient on the English table.

It is possible to buy yogurt from small dairies or to make your own using unpasteurized milk for preference. Powdered cultures can be bought from specialist laboratories and armed with these, one can make a batch of cultures to last a season — they keep quite well in the deep freeze. Alternatively, make it using a bought pot of live yoghurt as a starter and buy a new pot when the taste of the yogurt becomes too sharp.

Yogurt is often used as a light alternative to cream, especially soured cream, in sauces, soups and stuffings. It also makes delicious puddings and is, of course, the other cohabitee of the muesli belt.

Figs Stuffed with Yogurt

Serve these little sweetmeats with coffee after a special meal or as an alternative to a formal pudding.

SERVES: 6
DRIPPING TIME: several hours *or* overnight
PREPARATION TIME: 10 minutes
CHILLING TIME: 2 hours

285ml (½ pint) thick goat's yogurt
18 dried or fresh figs

1 Drain the yogurt in a muslin bag for several hours or overnight.
2 Cut a slit in each fig and fill the body of the fruit with the firm yogurt, rounding out the skin to make a good shape.
3 Chill for at least 2 hours before serving.

LABNA WITH HONEY AND NUTS

SERVES: 6
SOAKING TIME: OVERNIGHT
DRIPPING TIME: SEVERAL HOURS
PREPARATION TIME: MINIMAL

850ml (1½ pints) thick goat's yogurt
18 Hunza apricots, macerated overnight in water
clear honey
toasted flaked almonds and hazelnuts

1 Hang up the yogurt in a muslin bag and leave to drip for several hours.
2 To serve, spoon layers of the yogurt cheese (labna) into wine glasses, alternating with layers of dribbled honey, apricots and toasted nuts.

PRALINE

Crisp caramelized almond praline is a wonderful store cupboard standby. It can be incorporated into ice cream and sweetmeats, coffee or custard creams, or used to decorate cakes and biscuits. Praline also provides a foil to the soft fruitiness of orange and apple puddings.

MAKES: 455g (1 lb) praline
COOKING TIME: approximately 30 minutes

225g (½ lb) unblanched almonds
225g (½ lb) unrefined demerara sugar
4 tablespoonsful water

1 Put the almonds, sugar and water in a heavy-based saucepan over a low heat and allow the sugar to melt. Increase the heat slightly and stir the almonds round so they are thoroughly coated with the melted sugar. Continue to cook until the mixture is a dark, bubbling brown colour and it begins to smell strongly of caramel. Remove from the heat and tip out onto a greased or aluminium foil-lined baking sheet and leave to set.
2 When the praline is cold, crush with a rolling pin into usable-sized pieces and store in an airtight tin until needed.

EGGS

As Valentine's Day indicates, the birds start Spring early and by March the chickens are laying well in readiness for Easter. Custard is an almost notorious English favourite and made with the finest fresh milk and eggs it is unsurpassed.

Eggs should be gathered from hens living in relatively unconfined quarters with access to green grass and herbs. This gives the yolks their glorious yellow colour and definitive flavour. Cooking with such eggs is a joy and it makes the cook's task simple when the whites billow firmly after a moment of whisking and the yolks impart a depth and particular richness to custards and sauces for which nothing can be substituted.

Baked custards can be flavoured with vanilla, bay leaves or orange and chocolate, framed with vivid, pure tasting fruit sauces, and decorated with any small flowers that take the cook's eye in the garden. I like to make mine in little moulds and turn them out for a more three dimensional effect but they taste as delicious set in pretty glass cups.

BAKED CUSTARD WITH
CARAMEL CREAM AND PRALINE

SERVES: 6
PREPARATION TIME: 10 minutes
COOKING TIME: About 10 minutes for the caramel
BAKING TIME: 30 minutes

	CARAMEL CREAM
425ml (¾ pint) fresh milk (goat's milk is especially good)	115g (4 oz) unrefined demerara sugar
1 vanilla pod or a few drops of natural vanilla essence	140ml (¼ pint) water
	180ml (6 fl oz) fresh double cream
3 large free-range eggs, plus 1–2 extra egg yolks (optional)	Praline (page 46) and fresh whipped cream to serve
1 tablespoonful unrefined demerara sugar	

1 First make the custard. Grease 6 oval dariole moulds with a light, tasteless oil such as sunflower.

2 In a small saucepan over very low heat, infuse the milk with the vanilla pod for 10 minutes.

3 Preheat the oven to 300°F/150°C/Gas mark 2.

4 Beat the eggs and sugar together with a fork, pour in the warm milk into the egg mixture, mix well and strain into the moulds. Bake in a water bath for 30 minutes, or until the custards are set. Remove from the oven and keep in a cool place.

5 While the custards are baking, make the caramel cream. In a heavy-based saucepan, dissolve the sugar in the water over a low heat. Increase the heat, bring to the boil and continue boiling until the mixture is very dark and puffing like a volcano. Remove from the heat.

6 Pour the cream into the caramel, stirring all the time, until the sauce is smooth and glossy.

7 To unmould the custards, run a thin knife round the edges of the moulds, invert onto a plate and shake carefully. Place a spoonful of whipped cream beside each custard, swirl over some caramel cream and scatter with praline to give an interesting contrast in texture.

TANSY

Tansies take their name from the herb tansy, a feathery-leaved, verdant plant sporting small, yellow, button-like flowers with a pungent scent reminiscent of chrysanthemums. Tansy was one of the first strewing herbs used in Elizabethan times to keep floors smelling sweet and free from flies. It also appears in many 16th- and 17th-century recipes using eggs and milk and as a flavouring for Easter cakes — a reminder of the biblical 'bitter herbs' at Passover. Gradually the herb was omitted as an ingredient, but the name persisted. Tansy is a hardy perennial and an easy, attractive plant to grow in the garden. The flavour in the first of my tansy recipes is taken from the herb's juice (although coloured by green-tinged spinach) and is strange to our modern palates. In the second recipe, only the name lingers on.

TANSY CUSTARD

SERVES: 6
COOKING TIME: 5 minutes
PREPARATION TIME: 20 minutes
BAKING TIME: 30 minutes

225g (½ lb) fresh spinach leaves
approximately 12 tansy leaves
3 free-range eggs, plus 1 extra egg yolk
140ml (¼ pint) fresh single cream
140ml (¼ pint) fresh milk
1 tablespoonful unrefined golden granulated sugar
freshly grated nutmeg
140ml (¼ pint) fresh orange juice

1 Wash the spinach thoroughly and put the damp leaves into a saucepan. Cook lightly, remove from the heat and allow to cool. Squeeze out the juice into a bowl. The best way is to use your hands. You will need 3–4 tablespoonsful. Discard the spinach pulp.

2 Wash the tansy leaves and put them, damp, into a liquidizer with 1 tablespoonful water and whizz briefly. Squeeze out the juice by pressing the green pulp round in a nylon sieve into a bowl with a wooden spoon. (You can use the bowl containing the spinach juice.) Discard the tansy pulp.

3 Beat together the eggs, cream, milk, sugar, nutmeg, spinach and tansy juices.

4 Preheat the oven to 300°F/150°C/Gas mark 2.

5 Oil 6 dariole moulds or a custard mould or ovenproof bowl and fill with the custard mixture. Bake in a water bath for about 30 minutes, or until the custards are set. Remove from the oven and set aside to cool.

6 When cool, slip a knife round the custards and turn out onto individual plates. Pour a little orange juice around the pale green custards or serve separately if you have baked the pudding in a bowl or custard mould.

APPLE TANSY

I found this recipe in a 17th-century Herefordshire recipe book. The browned apple rings embossed in the sweet omelette make this simple pudding very attractive.

SERVES: 4–6
PREPARATION TIME: 10 minutes
COOKING TIME: 10 minutes

4 dessert apples, such as May Queen
45g (1½ oz) unsalted butter
squeeze of lemon juice
4 free-range eggs
1 tablespoonful unrefined demerara sugar
ground cinnamon
freshly grated nutmeg
thick Jersey cream to serve

1 Peel, core and slice the apples into rings. Melt 30g (1 oz) of the butter in a frying pan and sauté the apples until soft, about 5 minutes. Sprinkle with lemon juice and set aside in the pan.
2 Whisk the eggs in a bowl with the sugar and plenty of cinnamon and nutmeg.
3 Return the pan containing the apple rings to the heat, adding the remaining butter to lubricate the apples. When the butter is foaming, tip in the egg mixture. When the omelette has set on the underside, hold a plate over the pan and turn the omelette over to brown the other side. Remove from the heat.
4 Serve warm, cut into wedges, with thick Jersey cream.

SPRING MENUS

SIMPLE SUPPER

Seakale Wrapped in Ham (page 31)
Pan Haggerty (page 24)

Chicory and Orange Salad (page 171)

Apple Tansy (page 51)

VEGETARIAN SUPPER OR LIGHT LUNCH

Asparagus Pancakes (page 19)
Green Garlic Potatoes (page 23)

Carrot and Apple Salad (page 29)

Labna with Honey and Nuts (page 46)
Fresh Fruit

DINNER PARTY

Sorrel Soup (page 15)

Salmon Tail Tartlets (page 21)

Herefordshire Beef Olives in Cider Sauce (page 36)
Cauliflower with Toasted Sesame Seeds (page 119)
Carrots with Mustard Sauce (page 30)
Soufflé Potatoes (page 28)

Chocolate Cheesecake (page 44)
Rhubarb and Honey Jelly (page 40)

SUMMER

With the advent of the warmth of Summer, the cook can at last relax, although the cook's and the calendar's Summers do not quite coincide. Midsummer is still an early date in the garden, though sweet young vegetables are now beginning to arrive at the kitchen door.

Now most of the planting out has been completed and the gardener turns his attention to the tending of the rapidly-growing young plants — watering, weeding, staking and the first harvestings. The garden still looks orderly, until the rampant growth of late summer begins to overtake it. The fruit on the trees begin to swell; small excess apples fall in the June drop.

Early beetroot, peas, broad beans and new potatoes, and a little later, young courgettes delight the eye and palate. Now is the time to lay aside the casserole and saucepan and rely on the simple, delicate flavours of the young crops and fragrance of the herbs.

Salads almost look after themselves — a few delicious lettuce hearts and some herbs to hand, served with a light dressing and perhaps some flowers for garnish.

In the warmer weather, soft fruits provide the perfect pudding with their brilliant jewel colours and fresh sparkling tastes, the ideal excuse for a bowl of thick cream or a spoonful of crumbly curd.

BEETROOT SOUP

A ruby-red soup for summer, equally delicious hot or cold, with a hint of spice.

SERVES: 6
PREPARATION TIME: 30 minutes
COOKING TIME: 30 minutes
CHILLING TIME: (optional) 4 hours

I large onion, peeled and chopped
3 cloves garlic, chopped
900g (2 lb) unpeeled raw beetroot, chopped
1.1 litres (2 pints) water
juice of ½ lemon, or to taste
1–2 teaspoonful unrefined demerara sugar to taste
I teaspoonful whole allspice berries
sea salt
2 egg yolks, beaten
fresh English parsley to garnish
2 tablespoonful natural yogurt to garnish (if serving chilled)

1 Put the onion, garlic and beetroot in a large saucepan with the cold water, bring to the boil and simmer steadily for 20 minutes. Remove from the heat.

2 Strain off the liquid into a bowl, pressing down on the vegetable pulp with a wooden spoon to extract all the goodness. Discard the vegetable pulp and add the lemon juice and sugar.

3 Crush the allspice berries with a pestle and mortar and add to the soup. Season with salt to taste. Pour a ladleful of soup over the eggs and whisk well together. Return the mixture to the rinsed out saucepan and reheat carefully. Do not allow it to boil at this stage or the eggs will curdle instead of gently thickening and enriching the soup.

4 If you prefer a smooth soup, sieve out the grains of allspice. Garnish with flecks of bright green parsley.

5 This soup is also marvellous chilled, in which case swirl in a spoonful of yogurt before serving.

LANDCRESS AND LETTUCE SOUP

Landcress has a stronger and more peppery flavour than watercress, but it is easier to grow in the garden and combines well with the smoother taste of lettuce making this a thrifty way of using up the outer leaves of lettuce. The soup looks delightfully summery – pale green, flecked with darker speckles – and can be served chilled if the weather is hot. In this case make it with half whey or milk to half chicken stock, so the liquid does not set.

SERVES: 6
COOKING TIME: 20 minutes
PREPARATION TIME: 10 minutes
CHILLING TIME (optional): 4 hours

55g (2 oz) unsalted butter
I small onion, peeled and chopped
I small potato, peeled and sliced
I lettuce or outer leaves of 2 lettuces
1.1 litres (2 pints) hot chicken stock
2 handfuls landcress
sea salt
freshly ground black pepper
3 tablespoonsful fresh double cream
toasted almond flakes to garnish

1 Melt the butter in a large saucepan over a low heat and cook the onion until it is transparent, about 5 minutes. Add the potato slices and cook for a further 2 minutes. Pile in the lettuce leaves, which will quickly wilt. Add the chicken stock, bring to the boil and boil until the potato is cooked, 10–15 minutes. Remove from the heat and allow to cool slightly. Liquidize and strain.

2 Wash the landcress thoroughly as it grows low to the ground and is usually muddy. Tear off the leaves and put them into the liquidizer. Pour the strained soup on top of the landcress and whizz until the soup has turned a speckled green.

3 Return to the rinsed out saucepan and reheat. Stir in the seasoning and cream just before serving. Garnish with toasted almond flakes.

CUCUMBER AND FENNEL SOUP

This is another soup with a cool, green taste which can be served either hot or chilled. To serve chilled, replace half the chicken stock with either whey or buttermilk, traditionally used in refreshing summer drinks.

SERVES: 6

PREPARATION TIME: 10 minutes

COOKING TIME: 30 minutes

CHILLING TIME (optional): 4 hours

55g (2 oz) unsalted butter
3 shallots, peeled and finely chopped
1 Florence fennel bulb, sliced
1 cucumber, peeled and chopped into 1.25cm (½ inch) chunks
850ml (1½ pints) hot chicken stock
1 teaspoonful fennel seeds
sea salt
freshly ground black pepper
2 tablespoonsful natural yogurt
fennel fronds or cucumber croûtons to garnish

1 Melt the butter in a medium-sized saucepan over a low heat, add the shallots and 1 tablespoonful of water and cook for 10 minutes. Add the fennel, reserving the feathery fronds for garnish and cook for a further 10 minutes, then add the cucumber and chicken stock, increase the heat and cook for a further 5 minutes. Remove from the heat and allow to cool slightly.

2 Whizz the dry fennel seeds in a liquidizer to release their aroma, then tip in the soup mixture and purée together. Return to the rinsed out saucepan, season and reheat for 5 minutes to allow the fennel seeds to impart their strength to the soup.

3 Serve hot or chilled, either leaving the soup rough-textured, punctuated with seeds, or sieve for a smoother effect.

4 Just before serving, stir in the yogurt and garnish with snippets of fennel frond or dice the cucumber to make tiny raw croûtons to scatter over the surface.

SALMON MOUSSE WITH TARRAGON DRESSING

This is a nice way of presenting a small piece of leftover salmon. It will make ten little dariole moulds for the first course of a dinner party, or a light dish for summer lunch. The stock is made from the cooking liquor of the salmon, possibly poached in white wine, or from bringing the bits and pieces of skin and bone very slowly to the simmering point with wine, water and herbs and then straining off the liquid.

SERVES: 10 as starter, 6 as a main lunch dish
PREPARATION TIME: 10 minutes
SETTING TIME: 2 hours

3 leaves gelatine
285ml (½ pint) warm salmon stock
680g (1½ lb) cooked wild salmon
sea salt
freshly ground black pepper

TARRAGON DRESSING

5 tablespoonsful virgin olive oil
1 tablespoonful cider vinegar
1 tablespoonful fresh chopped French tarragon
Freshly grated nutmeg
sea salt
freshly ground black pepper
few whole tarragon leaves to garnish

1 Soften the gelatine in a little cold water, then dissolve it in the warm salmon stock. Then process this with 565g (1¼ lb) salmon and the seasoning. Flake the remaining salmon and stir into the purée.
2 Spoon into 10 lightly oiled dariole moulds or 1 large mould. Set aside until firm.
3 Turn out by running a thin, sharp knife round the moulds, or holding a hot, damp cloth briefly over the metal.
4 Make the dressing. Process all the ingredients except for the whole tarragon leaves, which will make a pretty garnish, and serve.

TONGUE SPICED WITH GREEN PEPPERCORNS WITH APPLE AND HORSERADISH SAUCE

Choose a pink tongue and use fresh horseradish for a really vibrant taste, nicely tempered with the apple and cream. Horseradish is a prolific plant and can be found in most old gardens and country lanes.

SERVES: 6
SOAKING TIME: several hours
COOKING TIME: 2 hours
COOLING TIME: 30 minutes
PREPARATION TIME: 30 minutes
CHILLING TIME: 2 hours

1 ox tongue, about 1.4kg (3 lb)
2 teaspoonsful green peppercorns
115g (4 oz) unsalted butter
freshly grated nutmeg

APPLE AND HORSERADISH SAUCE

1 cooking apple, peeled, cored and sliced
30g (1 oz) horseradish root
3 tablespoonsful fresh double cream
6 small tomatoes to serve
crushed green peppercorns and sprigs of fresh
salad burnet to garnish

1 Soak the tongue in cold water for several hours to remove the salt. Drain.
2 Put the tongue in a large saucepan, cover with fresh water, bring to the boil and simmer for 2 hours. Remove from the heat, pour away the cooking liquor – it has no quality for stock – and allow the tongue to cool. While the tongue is cooking, put the apple for the sauce into a small saucepan and cook to a pulp. Remove from the heat and reserve.
3 Skin the tongue, discarding any gristle and fat and chop the meat into 2.5cm (1-inch) dice. Crush the peppercorns with a pestle and mortar. Warm the butter in a small saucepan until it is almost melted.
4 Process the tongue, peppercorns, butter and nutmeg until fairly smooth – a little rough- ness makes the texture more interesting. Pack into a .5kg (1lb) oiled loaf tin, covered with

aluminium foil and chill in the refrigerator for about 2 hours or until set.

5 Make the sauce. Peel the horseradish root, this can sting the eyes more than peeling onions, and grate finely in a food processor. Whip the cream until thick and add to the horse-radish with the reserved apple pulp.

6 Unmould the tongue onto a serving plate by wrapping the tin in a hot cloth for a few seconds or running the blade of a thin, sharp knife around the edge of the tin.

7 Decorate with a patterned trail of crushed green peppercorns and sprig of salad burnet. The horseradish sauce looks pretty in a tomato cup.

CALLAMINCO

I have taken this recipe from an old Herefordshire cookery book. Spiced, potted tongue is elaborated with layers of pounded chicken, which makes a pretty dish for a summer lunch, served perhaps with beetroot and pineapple salad in a bowl lined with lettuce and sorrel leaves and with some potato mayonnaise.

This is the old recipe: 'Take cold tongue and beat it as fine as you can. Season it with a little black pepper, nutmeg, cloves and mace. Pour in a little clarified butter as you beat it. Then take the meat of a fowl and season it with salt, nutmeg, cloves and mace to your taste and beat it by itself. Pour in a little clarified butter as you beat it. Then put a layer of tongue, then of fowl till the pot is full. Pour clarified butter on top.'

Lettuce and Pea Soufflé

This soufflé can be served either as a starter, or as a surprisingly tasty vegetarian main course, in which event, use 15cm (6-inch) soufflé dish and bake for 35 minutes.

Serves: 8 as a starter or 4 as a main course
Preparation time: 15 minutes
Cooking time: 25 minutes
Baking time: 10–35 minutes (see above)

45g (1½ oz) unsalted butter
85g (3 oz) wholemeal breadcrumbs
225g (½ lb) lettuce leaves (the outer leaves can be useful for this)
565g (1¼ lb) fresh peas in the pod, shelled
1 small onion, peeled and halved
1 bay leaf
140ml (¼ pint) fresh milk
30g (1 oz) wholemeal flour
5 free-range eggs, separated
1 tablespoonful freshly grated Parmesan cheese

1 Butter the ramekins or soufflé dish with 15g (½ oz) of the butter and line with breadcrumbs to prevent the soufflés from sticking to the sides as they rise. Save the remaining breadcrumbs for the tops.
2 Wash the lettuce leaves and put them, still damp, into a medium-sized saucepan over a low heat to 'melt'. Set aside.
3 Cook the peas briefly in very little water, remove from the heat and drain.
4 Put the onion, bay leaf and milk in a small saucepan and bring to simmering point. Remove from the heat and allow to infuse for about 10 minutes. Remove the onions and bay leaf.
5 Drain the lettuce of any excess moisture and process with the peas and flavoured milk.
6 Melt the remaining butter in a medium-sized saucepan over a low heat, stir in the flour and cook for 1 minute. Add the lettuce and pea purée to make a sauce. Cook for about 2 minutes, remove from the heat and allow to cool. Beat the egg yolks into the mixture.
7 Preheat the oven to 400°F/200°C/Gas mark 6.

8 Whip up the egg whites until stiff and fold them carefully into the soufflé base with a metal spoon. Fill the prepared ramekins or soufflé dish loosely level, mix the reserved bread-crumbs and Parmesan cheese together, sprinkle on top and bake the ramekins for 10 minutes or the soufflé dish for 35 minutes. Serve immediately.

LOVAGE SOUFFLÉ

Soufflés need a strong taste to permeate the light froth of the eggs. Lovage gives a wonderful, heady aroma, which greets you when the oven door is opened.

SERVES: 8 as a starter
PREPARATION TIME: 15 minutes
COOKING TIME: 10 minutes
BAKING TIME: 10 minutes

45g (1½ oz) unsalted butter
85g (3 oz) wholemeal breadcrumbs
bunch of fresh lovage leaves, to taste
30g (1 oz) wholemeal flour
285ml (½ pint) fresh milk
5 large free-range eggs, separated
2 tablespoonsful fresh finely grated Parmesan cheese
sea salt
freshly ground black pepper

1 Butter 8 individual ramekins with 15g (½ oz) of the butter and line with breadcrumbs to prevent the soufflé from sticking to the sides as they rise. Save the remaining breadcrumbs for the tops.

2 In a small saucepan, melt the butter over a low heat, then add the lovage leaves. When they are wilted, stir in the flour and cook for 1 minute. Gradually add the milk to make a sauce. Remove from the heat.

3 Whizz the lovage mixture in a processor until it is spotted green. Cool, then incorporate the egg yolks, half the Parmesan cheese and the seasoning. The mixture should be fairly runny.

4 Preheat the oven 425°F/220°C/Gas mark 7.

5 Whisk the egg whites until stiff. Fold them carefully into the soufflé base with a metal spoon and fill the prepared ramekins loosely level. Mix the remaining breadcrumbs and Parmesan cheese together and sprinkle over the tops.

6 Bake the soufflés for 10 minutes, or until they are nicely risen and still slightly moist in the middle. Serve immediately.

BEETROOT AND CURD CHEESE

Sweet young beetroot and curd, enlivened with poppyseeds and the briskness of chopped chives, make a very simple and pretty starter.

SERVES: 6
PREPARATION TIME: 10 minutes
COOKING TIME: 45 minutes–1 hour

6 small beetroot
340g (¾ lb) curd cheese (see page 42)
1 teaspoonful poppy seeds
1 tablespoonful chopped fresh chives
sea salt
lemon juice
fresh English parsley or chive flowers to garnish

1 Twist the tops off the beetroot and wash them carefully without piercing the skin. This stops them 'bleeding' and losing their flavour. Steam until tender, about 45 minutes–1 hour, cool and the slip off the skins.
2 Work the curd gently with a fork until it is fluffy and light. Add the poppy seeds and chives and salt to taste.
3 Slice each beetroot into 5 or 6 rings. Arrange them in a circle on a small plate, just over-lapping like petals and brush with lemon juice. Heap the curd lightly in the centre and garnish with parsley or chive flowers.

PRAWNS GRILLED WITH FENNEL

A light starter or supper dish – the crunchy vegetable setting off the sweet, succulence of the prawns in summery colours of pink and green. Frozen prawns will do in an emergency but really only the best grade of Atlantic prawns are worthwhile.

SERVES: 6 as a starter or 4 as a supper dish
PREPARATION TIME: 10 minutes
COOKING TIME: 10 minutes
GRILLING TIMES: 10 minutes

340g (12 oz) fresh cooked prawns, shelled
1 large Florence fennel bulb

FENNEL SAUCE

2 cloves garlic
sea salt
55g (2 oz) unsalted butter
30g (1 oz) wholemeal flour
½ pint fennel stock (see below)
juice of ½ lemon
120ml (4 fl oz) fresh single cream
2 teaspoonsful Pernod (optional)
freshly ground black pepper
3 tablespoonsful wholemeal breadcrumbs
finely grated farmhouse Cheddar cheese
lemon slices to garnish

1 Slice the fennel thinly into small sections about 1.25cm (½-inch) long, reserving any bright green fronds. Blanch quickly in boiling water until just slightly crunchy. Drain and put on one side, reserving the cooking water which is the fennel stock.
2 To make the sauce, mash the garlic with the sea salt in a pestle and mortar. Scrape into a medium-sized saucepan and cook briefly in the butter over a low heat. Raise the heat slightly and stir in the flour. Cook for 1 minute, than add the fennel stock to make a sauce. When it has thickened, stir in the lemon juice, cream and Pernod, if using it.

3 Heat the grill to medium–high. Arrange the prawns and fennel slices in 6 shallow oven-proof dishes. Divide the sauce between them and scatter with the breadcrumbs and cheese.
4 Grill for 10 minutes, until the sauce is brown and bubbling.
5 Decorate with fresh fennel fronds and slices of lemon and serve with chunks of wholemeal bread and butter.

EELS

Eels may be caught in the Severn and Wye and in the many tributaries and brooks run-
ning through the countryside. My fishmonger in Hereford tells me when he has some —
supplies are irregular and unpredictable and I always seize the opportunity of cooking
eels as an interesting and tasty first course.

Eels, like all fish, must be as fresh as possible (still alive when they are delivered to the
shop or kitchen). Make sure though that they are truly freshly caught and have not been
lingering in an eel keep, under stress and losing condition. I confess that I ask my
fishmonger to skin them for me.

FRIED EELS WITH FRIED PARSLEY AND BACON

SERVES: 6 as a starter
PREPARATION TIME: 10 minutes
COOKING TIME: 20 minutes

680g (1½ lb) fresh eels, approximately 2.5cm (1 inch)
in diameter, skinned and gutted
3 tablespoonsful wholemeal flour, seasoned with sea salt and
freshly ground black pepper
3 tablespoonsful cold pressed olive oil
6 rashers unsmoked back bacon
6 well-shaped fresh English parsley sprigs, about
10cm (4 inches) long
570ml (1 pint) sunflower oil for deep-frying

1 Cut the eels into 7.5cm (3-inch) sections and coat with the seasoned flour.
2 Heat the olive oil in a large frying pan over a moderate heat and fry the eels gently, until
they are browned and the meat is just beginning to part from the bones, about 7 minutes.
This will probably have to be done in two batches. Remove the eels from the frying pan and
keep warm.

3 Cut the rinds off the bacon and grill until crisp. Keep warm.

4 Heat the sunflower oil in a heavy-based pan and drop in the parsley sprigs, two by two into the hot oil. Be careful to let them dry off first if you have had to wash them. The sprigs will explode and crackle excitingly when they are dropped into the oil because of their own inherent moisture. As soon as the parsley sprigs have stiffened, but are still dark green, fish them out with a slotted spoon. They will now be exceedingly brittle, so lay them tenderly on some absorbent kitchen paper to drain.

5 Serve the eels and bacon with the Victorian fernlike parsley garnish.

EELS FILLETED WITH PARSLEY SAUCE

SERVES: 6 as a starter
PREPARATION TIME: 30 minutes
COOKING TIME: 15 minutes

	PARSLEY SAUCE
2 shallots	milk reserved from poaching eels
425ml (¾ pint) fresh milk	2 teaspoonsful arrowroot
I bay leaf	sea salt
6 whole black peppercorns	freshly grated nutmeg
several stalks of fresh English parsley	2 tablespoonsful chopped fresh English parsley
900g (2 lb) fresh eels, skinned and gutted	lemon slices to garnish

1 Roughly chop the shallots and put into a small saucepan with the milk, bay leaf, peppercorns and parsley stalks. Bring this slowly to the boil, remove from the heat and infuse for 10 minutes to allow the flavours to steep, then strain off the liquid and reserve.

2 Fillet the eels – fiddly, but greatly appreciated by the recipients – and cut into 10cm (4-inch) lengths. Briefly poach in the infused milk over a gentle heat, then keep moist and warm in a little of the poaching liquid.

3 Make a white sauce with the remainder of the infused milk and arrowroot, but do not allow the sauce to boil. Season with salt and nutmeg and scatter with the parsley.

4 Coat the eels with the sauce, garnish with lemon slices and serve with wholemeal buns and butter.

EELS AND PRUNES AND BACON

This is a richer dish than the previous two as might be expected with its French origins.

SERVES: 6 as a starter
SOAKING TIME: several hours
PREPARATION TIME: 10 minutes
COOKING TIME: 15 minutes
BAKING TIME: 30 minutes

425ml (¾ pint) dry white wine or dry cider
6 large Californian prunes or 12 smaller ones
680g (1½ lb) fresh eels, skinned and gutted
1 tablespoonful cold pressed olive oil
115g (4 oz) streaky bacon, chopped into 5cm (2-inch) lengths
2 cloves garlic
sea salt
2 egg yolks
3 tablespoonsful fresh double cream

1 Pour enough wine or cider over the prunes to cover and leave to soak until soft.

2 Chop the eels into 2.5cm (1-inch) sections.

3 Heat the oil in a large frying pan and fry the bacon pieces until crisp. Lift them out with a slotted spoon, then brown the eels in the same oil. Remove from the pan.

4 Preheat the oven to 300°F/150°C/Gas mark 2. Fit the eels in a small casserole, with the prunes and soaking liquid, the bacon, remaining wine or cider and the garlic, crushed with a little salt. Remember that the bacon will impart some saltiness. Cook for 30 minutes.

5 Remove the casserole from the oven, strain off the cooking liquid into a saucepan and reduce to 285ml (½ pint). Off the heat, whisk in the egg yolks and cream.

6 Arrange the eels, prunes and bacon on small heated dishes, ladle a little sauce over and serve.

TURBOT BAKED IN A SAGE SAUCE

Turbot is a treat for us in landlocked Herefordshire. I once forgot to ask my fishmonger to fillet it for me and this enormous fish arrived, the size of a shield! Large kitchens used to have specially capacious turbot pans in which to lay these fish whole, but for most people filleting is the answer. Turbot is a kingly fish and like salmon, there are plans to farm it, which unfortunately seems to mean that it may lose in quality what it gains in availability.

SERVES: 6
PREPARATION TIME: minimal
COOKING TIME: 15 minutes
BAKING TIME: 25 minutes

SAGE SAUCE	sea salt
55g (2 oz) unsalted butter	freshly ground black pepper
8 shallots, finely chopped	900g (2 lb) skinned turbot fillets
2 tablespoonsful water	6 bantam or 12 quail eggs, hard-boiled and peeled
140ml (¼ pint) dry vermouth	wholemeal breadcrumbs
55g (2 oz) wholemeal flour	sprigs of fresh red or green sage for decoration
140ml (¼ pint) fish stock	
140ml (¼ pint) fresh single cream	
2 tablespoonsful chopped fresh green sage leaves	

1 First make the sauce. Melt half the butter in a medium-sized saucepan over a moderate heat, add the shallots and water and cook until softened, about 5 minutes. Add the vermouth and reduce to a sticky syrup. Put in the remaining butter, stir in the flour and cook for 1 minute. Add the stock and cream and cook until thickened, stirring hard. Lower the heat slightly, bubble for 2 minutes, mix in the sage and season with salt and pepper. Remove from the heat.

2 Preheat the oven to 375°F/190°C/Gas mark 5.

3 Cut the turbot into 2.5cm (1-inch) chunks and fit into a baking dish with the hard-boiled eggs. Pour the sauce over, sprinkle with breadcrumbs and bake for 25 minutes.

4 Serve immediately, brightened with sprigs of red or green sage.

WHITING IN CIDER AND
LOVAGE SAUCE

Whiting is a lightly-flavoured fish which needs a boost. I find the intensity of lovage is just right.

SERVES: 6
COOKING TIME: 15 minutes

6 whiting, filleted
285ml (½ pint) dry cider
170g (6 oz) unsalted butter, cut into pieces
sea salt
2 tablespoonsful chopped fresh lovage leaves
freshly ground black pepper
lemon twists to garnish

1 Preheat the oven to 250°F/130°C/Gas mark ½.

2 Put the whiting fillets in a large frying pan, cover with cider and bring to simmering point over a moderate heat. Simmer for 5 minutes, or until the fillets are cooked. Take them out carefully with a fish slice and keep warm on a serving plate in a low oven while you prepare the sauce.

3 Reduce the poaching liquid until it just covers the bottom of the pan. Then, off the heat, swirl in the butter piece by piece so that the sauce thickens. Stir in the lovage and season with salt and pepper.

4 Serve the fish, dressed with the sauce and garnished with lemon twists.

COURGETTES WITH ROSEMARY

This way with courgettes beautifully complements a plain poached salmon.

SERVES: 6
PREPARATION TIME: minimal
COOKING TIME: minimal

680g (1½ lb) fresh young courgettes
30g (1 oz) unsalted butter
120ml (4 fl oz) fresh double cream
1–2 sprigs fresh rosemary
sea salt
freshly ground black pepper

1 Cut the courgettes into slices about .25cm (⅛-inch) thick.
2 Blanch for 2–3 minutes in boiling water. Drain and refresh under cold running water. If the courgettes are exceptionally fresh and tender, you can omit this step.
3 When it is time to dish up, melt the butter in a saucepan over a moderate heat, tip in the courgettes, stir around for a moment, then add the cream and rosemary. Turn the courgettes over until warmed through in the bubbling sauce. Season to taste and remove the rosemary before serving.

SPICED RICE

Another of our favourite foods is rice, which can be boring just plain boiled. I like at least to toss it in a frying pan in a little olive oil for a few moments before serving. You can add, if you wish, a few flaked almonds, chopped chives or spring onion tops and a little spice, such as freshly ground cardamom, cumin or coriander. My husband likes to eat this on its own, but it is a good base for my Beef Stroganoff (page 75).

SERVES: 6

COOKING TIME: 20-25 minutes

340g (2 tea cups) brown long-grain Surinam rice
680ml (4 tea cups) stock or water
I bay leaf
I teaspoonful ground cumin
I teaspoonful ground coriander
I teaspoonful crushed cardamom seeds
celery salt
freshly ground green or black pepper
toasted flaked almonds
fresh chopped chives and parsley
3 tablespoonful cold pressed olive oil

1 Wash the rice, put it in a saucepan with the bay leaf and stock or water, bring to the boil over a moderate heat, then reduce the heat and cook for about 20 minutes, or until the rice is cooked, but still has a nice bite to it.

2 Strain off any remaining liquid and rinse under a hot tap.

3 Keep the rice warm in a steamer lined with greased foil while assembling the other ingredients.

4 Just before serving, gently heat the oil in a large frying pan, add the rice, seasoning, almonds and herbs and turn everything over in the oil to warm through.

My Beef Stroganoff

Chervil is the magic ingredient in this recipe. We grow it in the central propagating section of the greenhouse, where its frail filigree leaves fill the shady place beneath the staging with green.

SERVES: 6
PREPARATION TIME: 10 minutes
COOKING TIME: 10–15 minutes

680g (1½ lb) well-hung rump or fillet steak
30g (1 oz) unsalted butter
2 tablespoonsful cold pressed olive oil
225g (½ lb) onions, thinly sliced
225g (½ lb) fresh mushrooms thinly sliced
140ml (¼ pint) good beef stock or beef meat jelly
2 tablespoonsful Madeira (optional)
squeeze of lemon juice
sea salt
freshly ground black pepper
2–3 tablespoonsful chopped fresh chervil
cornflour to thicken sauce (optional)
90ml (3 fl oz) thick natural yogurt

1 Cut the beef into thin strips. About 4 x .5cm (1½ inches by ¼-inch).
2 In a large frying pan, melt the butter in the oil over a moderate heat and fry the onions for a few minutes until softened. Put them on one side to keep warm. Increase the heat, add the meat strips to the pan and brown quickly. Return the cooked onion to the pan. Add the mushrooms, stock or meat jelly and Madeira, if using it. Simmer for a few more minutes, then add the lemon juice, seasoning and chervil. If you prefer a slightly thicker sauce, strain off the juices, keeping the meat warm, and cook the liquid with a little cornflour mixed with cold water to a paste to bind it. Strain out any lumps before returning to the pan.
3 Finally, fold in the yogurt, which will melt and mingle with the meat juices. Serve on Spiced Rice.

TURKEY PILAF

This is my version of an age-old way of using up a turkey or any other feathered fowl. For a party, roast a bird specially. What really makes for success is the spicy sauce made of the meat juices from the roasting tin. If there is not enough, make up the amount with strong turkey or chicken stock.

SERVES: 6

PREPARATION TIME: 10 minutes

COOKING TIME: roasting the bird, plus 30 minutes

170g (6 oz) brown long-grain Surinam rice	**SAUCE**
1 bay leaf	240ml (8 fl oz) turkey meat jelly
570ml (1 pint) turkey stock	1 teaspoonful ground cumin
cold pressed olive oil	2 teaspoonful crushed coriander seeds
900g (2 lb) cooked turkey, cut into strips	1 teaspoonful freshly grated root ginger
	1 clove garlic, crushed with a little sea salt
	freshly ground black pepper
	cold pressed olive oil
	2 tablespoonsful chopped fresh chives
	55g (2 oz) toasted peanuts or flaked almonds
	sea salt
	fresh coriander leaves or English parsley, chopped

1 Wash the rice, put it in a saucepan with the bay leaf and stock and bring to the boil over a moderate heat. Reduce the heat and cook for about 20 minutes, or until the rice is cooked, but still has a nice bite to it.

2 Meanwhile, line a steamer with foil, brush it with olive oil and gently heat the turkey. Keep warm and covered.

3 Melt the meat jelly in a small saucepan over a moderate heat and stir in the cumin, coriander, ginger, garlic and seasoning. Simmer for five minutes, remove from the heat and set aside.

4 Just before serving, gently heat the oil in a large frying pan and tip in the cooked rice, chives, toasted nuts and sea salt. Turn the mixture around in the oil until heated through.

5 Arrange the turkey and rice on a large, warmed serving dish, moisten with the sauce and scatter over the coriander or parsley. Serve, handing round any extra sauce separately. Purple sprouting broccoli, spinach or a rich ratatouille are perfect partners for this dish.

RICE SALAD

Rice salad is a sort of cold version of spiced rice, good in early summer before the first potatoes start. It lends itself to a variety of interpretations. Served with a potent garlic mayonnaise and whatever herbs take your fancy, it is perfect for a warm summer evening's dinner in the garden, accompanied by a bottle of well-chilled Baron de L Pouilly Fumé, the Loire's best wine. Idyllic!

SERVES: 6–8

PREPARATION TIME: 10–15 minutes

COOKING TIME: 30 minutes

340g (2 tea cups) brown long-grain Surinam rice	**GARLIC MAYONNAISE**
680ml (4 tea cups) chicken stock or water	2 egg yolks
1 bay leaf	2–3 tablespoonsful cider vinegar
a little unsalted butter	285ml (½ pint) cold pressed olive oil
2 free-range eggs, beaten	3 cloves garlic, finely chopped
170g (6 oz) fresh peas and/or broad beans	pinch of English mustard powder
115g (4 oz) cooked fresh prawns and/or cooked	sea salt
sausage, diced	
170g (6 oz) black olives	
55g (2 oz) toasted flaked almonds	
fresh chopped herbs – chervil, tarragon, parsley,	
chives etc.	

1 Wash the rice and put it in a saucepan with the stock or water and the bay leaf and bring to the boil over a moderate heat. Reduce the heat and cook for 20 minutes, or until the rice is tender and the liquid has been absorbed. Tip the rice into a sieve and rinse under a cold tap. Set aside.

2 Melt the butter in a small frying pan, and make a thin omelette with the eggs. Cut this into strips.

3 Briefly cook the peas and/or beans in a little boiling water. Drain.

4 Make the mayonnaise in the usual manner.

5 Combine all the salad ingredients with the rice and serve the mayonnaise in a separate bowl or sauceboat.

TARRAGON BEEF

We grow French tarragon in the greenhouse perennially, where it flourishes for a long season. From early Spring to late Summer, the low green wave of delicate leaves brushes against the glass panes. Fresh tarragon is incomparable. Somehow its whole quality changes in drying.

SERVES: 6
PREPARATION TIME: minimal
COOKING TIME: 15–20 minutes

900g (2 lb) well-hung rump or fillet steak
2 tablespoonful cold pressed olive oil
285ml (½ pint) dry red wine
170g (6 oz) unsalted butter
2 tablespoonful chopped fresh tarragon
sea salt
freshly ground black pepper
fresh tarragon sprigs to garnish

1 Trim the steak and divide it into 6 portions.
2 Heat the oil in two heavy-based frying pans and fry the steaks according to degree or rareness desired. Remove the steaks from the pan and keep warm.
3 Tip out excess oil or fat from the pans. Divide the wine between the two pans and boil down over a moderately high heat, scraping up any brown bits, until there is only a couple of tablespoonsful of liquid in each pan. Remove from the heat.
4 Mash the tarragon into the butter with a fork. Whisk knobs of tarragon butter into the syrup juices in the pans until you have a thickened sauce. Season to taste, mix in any juices that have accumulated under the steaks and serve the sauce to one side of the steaks, garnished with a sprig of tarragon. New potatoes with butter and chives and young, pristine broad beans and carrots make this a feast.

SWEET PEPPERS

Sweet peppers are relatively new to our culinary landscape, but are now grown in many gardens and greenhouses in Summer as well as being important all year round. Imported peppers have the disadvantage of being rather thick skinned and dry, but the home-grown ones can be tender sweet and luscious.

Sweet peppers taste their best in partnership with their compatriots — tomatoes. Simmered together with onions and garlic until thick, and used to stuff pancakes or tart cases, the powerful flavour makes the aromatic aggrandizement of herbs unnecessary. A looser mixture makes a tangy sauce for pasta, scattered with freshly grated Parmesan cheese, and goes beautifully with chicken. Red peppers can also flavour and tint a mayonnaise or warm sauce — good with white fish.

STUFFED PEPPERS

This is a very nice dinner dish with hidden surprises. Try to choose peppers that are rather squat in shape, so they will balance upright.

SERVES: 6
PREPARATION TIME: 45 minutes
COOKING TIME: 30 minutes
BAKING TIME: 45 minutes

4 shallots chopped	**TOMATO AND BASIL SAUCE**
30g (1 oz) unsalted butter	455g (1 lb) tomatoes
115g (4 oz) brown long-grain Surinam rice	2 cloves garlic
340ml (2 tea cups) water or white wine	1 coffeespoonful sea salt
1 bay leaf	18 fresh basil leaves
115g (4 oz) lightly-toasted cashew nuts	2 tablespoonful virgin olive oil
6 red or green peppers	sea salt
1 tablespoonful chopped fresh thyme	freshly ground black pepper
1 tablespoonful chopped fresh English parsley	
sea salt	
freshly ground black pepper	
12–18 pine kernels	
6 large black olives, stoned	
6 large Californian prunes, stoned after cooking	
1 tablespoonful cold pressed olive oil	

1 Put the shallots, butter and a little water in a small saucepan over a moderate heat and cook until softened, about 5 minutes. Remove from the heat and set aside.

2 Wash the rice and put in a saucepan with the water or wine and the bay leaf and bring to the boil over a moderate heat. Reduce the heat to very low and cook for 20 minutes, or until the rice is cooked.

3 Meanwhile, preheat the oven to 400°F/200°C/Gas mark 6. Toast the cashew nuts until lightly browned, remove from the oven and set aside, but leave the oven on. Process the cashew nuts until they resemble fine breadcrumbs.

4 Cut the tops off the peppers to make lids and scoop out the seeds. If necessary, level the peppers by cutting a thin slice off the bottom so that they will stand upright. Mix the shallots, rice and cashew nuts together with the thyme, parsley and seasoning.

5 Pop 2 or 3 pine kernels into each olive and stuff one into each of the prunes.

Fill the peppers one-third full with the rice mixture, place a stuffed prune in each pepper, snugly fill with the remaining rice. Put on the lids, then fit the peppers into a casserole so they will stand upright, supporting each other. Brush with the oil, put 2 or 3 tablespoonsful of water in the bottom of the casserole and bake the peppers, uncovered, for about 45 minutes. Check after they have been baking for 30 minutes, as so much depends on the size and quality of the peppers.

6 While the peppers are in the oven, make the sauce. Cook the tomatoes until soft, then purée.

7 Crush the garlic with the salt in a pestle and mortar, add the basil and mash. Mix in the oil and add additional salt if required and pepper.

8 Heat the tomato purée in a saucepan over a low heat, then stir in the basil paste.

9 Pour a little sauce onto a warmed serving plate and set the peppers on it. One of the nicest vegetables to serve with this dish is cauliflower with toasted sesame seeds (page 119).

Chicken with Sweet Peppers

Serves: 6
Preparation time: 15 minutes
Cooking time: approximately 1 hour

6 tablespoonsful cold pressed olive oil
6 chicken portions, from a free-range chicken
1 medium-sized onion, cut into half moons
1 red pepper, finely sliced
1 green pepper, finely sliced
680g (1½ lb) tomatoes, roughly chopped
120ml (4 fl oz) dry white wine
3 gloves garlic
pinch of sea salt
1–2 tablespoonsful Hungarian paprika
arrowroot (optional)
90ml (3 fl oz) thick goat's yogurt at room temperature
extra paprika to garnish

1 Heat half the oil in a large frying pan and brown the chicken portions. Remove from the pan and keep warm.

2 Heat the remaining oil in the same pan and cook the onion and peppers until softened. Remove from the heat.

3 Meanwhile cook the tomatoes with the wine for about 10 minutes. Press through a sieve on top of the other vegetables. Add the garlic, crushed with the salt and paprika and mix well.

4 Arrange the chicken portions in a large covered saucepan, pour the vegetable sauce over and simmer, covered, for 35–45 minutes or until the chicken is tender. If the sauce is too thin, thicken it with a little arrowroot.

5 To serve, arrange the chicken and sauce on warmed serving plates, spoon over the yogurt giving a marbled effect and add a sprinkle of paprika. A dark green vegetable, such as spinach, and small potatoes steamed in their skins with butter and parsley are attractive accompaniments to this dish.

GLOBE ARTICHOKES

Of all the plants in the kitchen garden perhaps the globe artichokes are the most breath-takingly majestic, possessing great sculptural beauty.

Cook the artichokes by plunging them into boiling water. They are done when one of the lowest outer leaves will part easily from the stem.

They can be eaten hot, dipping each 'petal' into a dish of melted butter and sucking off the delicious fleshy morsel at the base of each leaf. Discard the spiky, thistly bit on top of the succulent heart which is the prize at the end of all that hard labour.

Or they can be eaten cold. Carefully open out the leaves, smaller artichokes may be cut through vertically, scoop out the whiskers and put a dollop of mayonnaise, studded with black olives perhaps or flavoured with herbs, in the cup. Prawns and crab are also perfect partners of artichokes and mayonnaise.

Sometimes the globes come in such disparate sizes that another approach is needed. Scrape off the flesh from the plumpest scales with a teaspoon and chop the 'meat' from the heart and mix it together with a little olive oil and cider vinegar dressing and some prawns, crab or other shellfish. Press this mixture into oiled dariole moulds. Turn them out and arrange four or five of the most beautiful scales, saved for this purpose, around the shapes. A little more dressing can be served alongside.

There are so many possible combinations. Another is to mix the chopped artichoke with a nut oil dressing, walnut or hazelnut are most easily available, and some chopped tomato and scented basil to make a filling for tomato cases. Remember to season the hollowed out tomato cases with sea salt and a grinding of black pepper beforehand.

TOMATO AND OATMEAL TART

A marvellous recipe of Jane Grigson's for a summer lunch when tomatoes are really plentiful and the sunshine has concentrated their intensity. The oatmeal pastry is a perfect foil for the rich tomato filling. This is an ideal dish to show off the superiority of home-grown tomatoes with superlative flavour.

SERVES: 6–8
PREPARATION TIME: 20 minutes
RESTING TIME: 20 minutes
COOKING TIME: 15 minutes
BAKING TIME: 30 minutes

OATMEAL PASTRY	TOMATO FILLING
115g (4 oz) wholemeal flour	55g (2 oz) unsalted butter
115g (4 oz) rolled organic porridge oats	1 medium-sized onion, chopped
pinch of sea salt	1 large clove garlic, chopped
115g (4 oz) unsalted butter	455g (1 lb) fresh ripe tomatoes, chopped
1 large free-range egg, beaten	1 free-range egg, beaten
	120ml (4 fl oz) fresh single cream
	1 heaped tablespoonful freshly grated Parmesan cheese
	55g (2 oz) farmhouse Cheddar cheese, grated
	few drops Tabasco sauce
	extra freshly grated Parmesan cheese

1 First make the pastry (see page 176) using the beaten egg to moisten it. Leave to rest for 20 minutes.

2 Meanwhile, melt the butter in a saucepan over a low heat. Add the onion and garlic and cook until soft, about 5 minutes. Remove from the heat.

3 In another saucepan, cook the tomatoes until soft. Remove from the heat and sieve them into the onion mixture. Cook hard until the mixture is thick, then set aside.

4 Beat the egg in a measuring jug with enough cream to make 140ml (¼ pint). Tip the cheeses and cream into the tomato mixture and stir in the Tabasco sauce. Taste to see if it is hot enough and adjust seasoning if necessary.

5 Put a baking sheet in the oven and preheat to 375°F/190°C/Gas mark 5.

6 Line a 22.5cm (9-inch) fluted flan tin with a removable base with the pastry. If it crumbles just patch it, it will not be noticed when it is baked.

Fill with the tomato mixture and sprinkle a little Parmesan cheese on top to give the tart extra colour when it is cooked.

7 Put the flan tin on the baking sheet and bake for 30 minutes, or until the tart is firm. Serve warm with a green salad. Perhaps a Webb's lettuce with strips of fennel, watercress or basil and pine nuts.

SALADS

I serve salads as a light refresher in the middle of a meal after a main course, though they stand equally well with cheese. For this reason I am not giving recipes for heftier salads which can be a whole meal in themselves. Many of the salad ideas can of course be adapted to make more substantial dishes with the addition of grated root vegetables, cooked pulses and potatoes and stronger ingredients like raw onion or leek.

I take a basic green salad ingredient for bulk. To lettuce, celery, chicory, cabbage, cucumber I add some background herbs such as sorrel, chives, chervil, salad burnet, parsley or purslane. I think it is a mistake to mix too many strongly flavoured herbs together and I try to use only one dominant herb in a salad, which could be lovage, basil, sweet marjoram or tarragon. This way one's tastebuds are not bombarded with a cacophany of disparate tastes.

Cucumber, fennel, cardoon, apple provide crunch as do toasted pinenuts, almonds, hazelnuts, walnuts and brazils, Sunflower seeds and roasted sesame seeds also add interest. But again I do not care to mix too many of these ingredients together. It is distracting and does not enhance the total effect.

Another dimension that harmonizes with the other ingredients of a salad is the addition of slices of firm fleshed fruits such as apple, pear and pineapple, juicier ones like oranges and grapes or raisins and sultanas. Again, choose with discretion and with regard to the dessert course of the meal.

The dressing of the salad is vitally important. I always use the best olive oil from the first cold pressing, or a nut oil. A lively dressing can spark up a dull salad. A distinctive oil like sesame oil is good used sparingly, or else take a mild, light or tasteless oil - sunflower for instance - and brighten it with herbs, honey or crushed spices to give exuberance and aromatic nuances. Or use yoghurt for variety and lightness.

The character of the dressing is also greatly influenced by the quality of the sharpening ingredient which is added to the oil. I use organic cider vinegar most of all but fresh citrus juice or good white wine vinegar work well according to the ingredients in the salad. Herb flavoured vinegars like tarragon and dill add extra vitality, especially if you can make them yourself.

To make the dressing, combine all the ingredients in a screw top jar and shake or whizz everything in a liquidizer. Do not dress the salad until you are ready to eat it or the green stuff will soon wilt.

Toss the salad in the dressing, preferably in a wooden bowl, and the ingredients will arrange themselves beautifully without any artifice. Sometimes, following tradition, drop one or two flower heads or petals of, say, chives, nasturtiums, marigolds into the salad to add gaiety and form.

LETTUCE AND GRAPEFRUIT SALAD

The grapefruit gives a delightfully refreshing edge to this salad and it may suit to cut down a little on the vinegar in the dressing.

SERVES: 6
PREPARATION TIME: 15 minutes

1 large Webb's lettuce
2–3 grapefruit
55g (2 oz) toasted flaked almonds
fresh watercress, to garnish

DRESSING

3 tablespoonsful green olive oil
1 teaspoonful cider vinegar

1 Separate the lettuce into leaves, wash, dry and tear into large bite-sized pieces.

2 Peel and segment the grapefruits. If the segments are large, halve them.

3 Make the dressing and toss with the lettuce, grapefruit and almonds in a salad bowl. Garnish with sprigs of watercress or a herb with an attractive leaf shape, such as salad burnet, Italian parsley or chervil.

CHEQUERED SALAD

I thought the combination of beetroot and pineapple – both wonderful ingredients – would be an interesting one for a late summer salad. It works, but the pineapple needs to be just at the right stage, sweet, but with just a toothsome sharpness about it.

SERVES: 6
PREPARATION TIME: 20 minutes
COOKING TIME: approximately 45 minutes

2 medium-sized beetroot
I fresh pineapple
115g (4 oz) shelled brazil nuts
I heaped tablespoonful English parsley, lightly cut

DRESSING

5 teaspoonsful virgin olive oil
I teaspoonful cider vinegar
freshly ground black pepper

1 Wash the beetroot without cutting off the root or crown as they will bleed and lose colour and flavour. Steam until tender, about 45 minutes. When cool, peel them and cut into 1.25cm (½-inch) dice.
2 Peel the pineapple, removing the 'eyes' with a sharp knife, and cube it correspondingly.
3 Cut the brazil nuts into three.
4 Make the dressing
5 Put the beetroot and pineapple into two separate bowls and divide the dressing between them, turning gently to mix. Add the nuts to the pineapple.
6 To serve, heap the pineapple and nuts in the centre of a serving bowl and arrange the beetroot in a ruff around the edge. Scatter with parsley to point up the colour.

HERB SALAD

A salad of infinite variety, in this case lifted by the luxurious addition of pine nuts and heartened by a distinctive nut oil. If you have no pine nuts handy, radishes, cut in little slices to resemble seaside rock, jolly up the green and add bite.

Nut oils are very concentrated. Some people prefer them diluted with a lighter oil. It is probably best to experiment.

SERVES: 6

PREPARATION TIME: 15 minutes

I large Webb's lettuce
I cucumber
several background herbs in season: chives, sorrel, parsley etc.
I dominant herb in season: tarragon, basil, lovage or sweet marjoram
85g (3 oz) pine kernels

DRESSING

3 tablespoonsful nut oil
2 teaspoonsful cider vinegar
pinch of sea salt
flowers to garnish

1 Separate the lettuce into leaves, wash and lay out to dry on a clean cloth or tea towel.

2 Peel the cucumber lengthways in about 5 downward strokes, leaving strips of skin between each cut to give a strip effect. Slice into thin rings and chill in the refrigerator.

3 When the lettuce is dry, tear into large, bite-sized pieces. Cut, snip or tear the herbs into small bits. For example, cut parsley and chives with scissors, but tear basil and sweet marjoram.

4 Make the dressing. When ready to serve, combine all the ingredients and strew with the herbs or garden flowers you have picked for decoration.

CUCUMBER AND APPLE MINT SALAD

An especially cooling salad with a double crunch factor. Try to use a dessert apple with a rosy skin like Scarlet Pimpernel which looks very pretty amongst the green and white.

SERVES: 6

PREPARATION TIME: 15 minutes

1 cucumber
85g (3 oz) hazelnuts, toasted and skinned
3–4 dessert apples (see above)
2 tablespoonsful chopped fresh apple mint
lemon juice (optional)

DRESSING

5 teaspoonsful hazelnut oil
1 teaspoonful cider vinegar
fresh apple mint sprigs and flowers to garnish

1 Peel the cucumber, scoop out any seeds and chop into 1.25cm (½-inch) dice. Cut the hazelnuts in half, vertically. Slice and core the apples – do not peel them – and cut into matching cubes.

2 Mix the oil and vinegar together and dress the salad immediately to prevent the apples browning, incorporating the chopped mint. Otherwise sprinkle the cut apples with a little lemon juice and dress later. This salad with stay crisp longer then a lettuce-based salad, which wilts very quickly after being dressed.

3 Decorate with mint sprigs and flowers.

LETTUCE AND COURGETTE SALAD

You only need a few young, tender courgettes for this salad – useful when there are not enough to pick for a full vegetable helping. Buttercrunch lettuce is, to my mind, supreme among lettuces in flavour and texture.

SERVES: 6
PREPARATION TIME: 10 minutes, plus another
minute to blanch the courgettes

1 Buttercrunch lettuce
6 small young courgettes, about 10cm (4-inches) long
landcress or sweet marjoram
sunflower seeds or toasted sesame seeds

DRESSING

6 tablespoonsful virgin olive oil
½ tablespoonful cider vinegar
1 teaspoon made English mustard
sea salt
freshly ground black pepper
fresh salad burnet to garnish

1 Separate the lettuce into leaves. Wash and dry by spreading the leaves out on a clean cloth or tea towel.

2 Cut the courgettes into rings about .25cm (⅛-inch) thick and blanch quickly in a very small amount of boiling water for 1 minute. Drain immediately and refresh under cold running water.

3 Just before serving, make the dressing, break the lettuce into large bite-size pieces and toss all the ingredients together.

DEMERARA MERINGUES

Using unrefined sugar makes for a richer flavoured meringue. I dry the demerara sugar in the oven 200°F/100°C/Gas mark 1 for an hour or two, then whizz in the blender. I try always to keep a storage jar of this fine sugar handy.

MAKES: approximately 32 meringues
PREPARATION TIME: 10 minutes
DRYING TIME: at least 3 hours

240ml (8 fl oz) egg whites
455g (1 lb) unrefined fine demerara sugar
light, tasteless oil to grease trays

1 Whisk the egg whites with an electric mixer on the highest setting until stiff. Spoon in two-thirds of the sugar with the motor still on high. Reduce the speed of the machine and add the remaining sugar.
2 Preheat the oven to 200°F/100°C/Gas mark 1. Oil two baking sheets and set out about 16 spoonfuls of meringue on each. Unless you can fit the two baking sheets side by side on the same shelf in the oven, put one baking sheet in the centre of the oven at 200°F/100°C/Gas mark 1 for 30 minutes. Then move this down to a lower position and put in the second. It will not harm the second tray of meringues to wait. After another 30 minutes lower the heat to 175°F/100°C/Gas mark ½ and continue cooking for at least another 2 hours. Change the baking sheets around to even up the cooking if necessary. When the meringues will slide off the trays with a rustle they are ready to eat or store in an airtight tin.
3 Serve sandwiched with fresh thick Jersey cream, surrounded by a strong fruit sauce made from puréed loganberries, raspberries, blackcurrants or strawberries.

VARIATIONS:
1 Marble the whipped cream with a little of the fruit sauce for a fetching effect and spoon a swag of darker sauce over each meringue half.
2 Fill the meringues with a thick chocolate and chestnut purée, and a dollop of thick whipped cream. Decorate with crumbled marrons glacés.

GREAT GRANNY'S VELVET CREAM

I always believed that my devout great-grandmother Maria was a firm supporter of the Temperance Movement, so I was surprised to find that many recipes in her little book included wines and spirits and indeed, recipes for alcoholic drinks. The following recipe is an example of a party pudding. I use a good medium-priced Sauternes like Château Bastor Lamontagne – a Cru Bourgeois – and stiffen the pudding with leaf gelatine, rather than the isinglass of the original recipe.

SERVES: 6

COOKING TIME: 10 minutes

PREPARATION TIME: minimal

SETTING TIME: 1–2 hours

140ml (¼ pint) sweet dessert wine
juice and carefully washed rind of ½ lemon
3 leaves gelatine
fine demerara sugar to taste (page 92)
285ml (½ pint) fresh double cream
lemon twists to decorate

1 Heat the wine with the lemon rind, juice and sugar in a saucepan over moderate heat and boil for 5 minutes. Remove from the heat, strain off the rind and set aside to cool.

2 Soften the gelatine in a little cold water and stir into the warm liquid until dissolved. Set aside.

3 Meanwhile, whip the cream lightly. When the mixture is beginning to thicken, fold in the cream. Pour the mixture into a wetted or greased mould or individual glasses and leave to firm up.

4 To serve, turn out onto a plate or serve in the glasses, decorated with lemon twists.

CHOCOLATE AND CINNAMON PARFAIT

Two chocolatey ideas combined from Helge Rubinstein's *Chocolate Book* – the light texture of the parfait and the spicy cinnamon flavour. Use the best quality bitter chocolate you can find.

SERVES: 8–10
COOKING TIME: 10 minutes
PREPARATION TIME: 10 minutes
FREEZING TIME: 2 hours

115g (4 oz) unrefined light muscovado sugar
140ml (¼ pint) water
1 cinnamon stick or ground cinnamon
115g (4 oz) bitter chocolate
1 tablespoonful strong brewed coffee
4 egg yolks
285ml (½ pint) fresh whipping cream
marigold petals, chamomile flowers or any tiny flowering
sprig to decorate

1 Put the sugar, water and cinnamon stick in a heavy saucepan and bring to the boil. When the sugar has dissolved, remove from the heat and stir in the chocolate. Set on one side and mix in the coffee.

2 Whisk the egg yolks with an electric whisk until they are light and creamy. Remove the cinnamon stick from the chocolate mixture and pour into the egg yolks.

3 Whip the cream until it just holds its shape, adding the ground cinnamon to taste if using it. Fold into the chocolate mixture and pour into individual ramekins. Put into the freezer to set, making sure they are level.

4 Remove from the freezer 5 minutes before serving and decorate with marigold petals, chamomile flowers or any tiny flowering sprig.

CREAM CURD HEARTS AND STRAWBERRIES

Whiter than white curd, slightly sweetened and moulded into heart shapes, bedecked with scarlet strawberries set on a green fig leaf makes one of the most visually dramatic puddings of the Summer. Other soft fruits, such as loganberries, raspberries, currants, mulberries or a combination of these are equally luscious. Ideally, this pudding should be eaten out of doors on a soft summer night.

SERVES: 2
PREPARATION TIME: 20 minutes
DRAINING TIME: overnight (optional)

fine unrefined demerara sugar to taste (page 92)
2 tablespoonsful fresh double cream (optional)
few drops natural vanilla essence
115g (4 oz) curd cheese (page 42)
fresh strawberries
fresh fig leaves or strawberry or mulberry leaves
extra double cream (optional)

STRAWBERRY SAUCE (optional)

extra strawberries, slightly sweetened
few drops lemon juice

1 Dissolve the sugar in the cream with the vanilla essence. Fork this lightly but thoroughly into the curd. Press into wetted individual china heart-shaped moulds. A real purist would line the moulds with muslin, fill them with curd strained from the preparing pan and leave them to drain overnight.

2 Place a fig leaf on each dessert plate and turn out a curd heart onto each one. Hull the strawberries and scatter around the curd. Drizzle a little more finely ground demerara sugar over the fruit and hand round extra cream to the greedy.

3 If you have plenty of strawberries, it is nice to make a sauce by whizzing strawberries in a blender or food processor, sweetening if necessary and possibly adding a little lemon juice. Spread the sauce around part of the edge of the curd heart to define its shape.

STRAWBERRY AND ORANGE JELLIES

Strawberry and orange is a classic combination. Choose really ripe, flavourful strawberries such as Royal Sovereign. Individual jellies are easier to serve, but set in a large bowl, this pudding is a brilliant centrepiece for the table.

SERVES: 6
PREPARATION TIME: 20 minutes
COOKING TIME: 5 minutes
CHILLING TIME: 2–3 hours

3 leaves gelatine
zest of I orange
425ml (¾ pint) fresh orange juice
3 tablespoonsful unrefined golden granulated sugar
juice of ½ lemon
few drops Angostura bitters
455g (I lb) fresh ripe whole strawberries
(cut in half if they are very large)
few drops of strawberry or raspberry eau de vie (optional)

ALMOND CREAM

I teaspoonful fine, unrefined demerara sugar (page 92)
180ml (6 fl oz) fresh double cream
1–2 drops natural almond essence
55g (2 oz) toasted flaked almonds to decorate
sprigs of fresh mint to decorate

1 Soak the gelatine in a little cold water. Scrub the orange skin thoroughly to remove any pesticides, fungicides or preservatives and grate the zest.
2 Put 140ml (¼ pint) of the orange juice in a saucepan with the orange zest and heat to a simmer over a moderate heat. Remove from the heat, stir in the sugar and allow to cool to blood heat.
3 Strain off the orange zest and stir in the softened gelatine until it has completely dissolved. Add the remaining orange juice, lemon juice and Angostura bitters to taste.
4 Sprinkle the strawberries and a few drops of eau de vie if you wish to intensify the flavour.
5 Divide half the orange mixture between 6 stemmed glasses, dropping in half the strawberries, whole, or halved if very large, or pour into a glass serving bowl. Chill in the

refrigerator to set for about 1 hour. When the jellies are firm, add the remaining juice and strawberries. Chill again to set this layer.

6 Dissolve the sugar in the cream and whip until just firm, stirring in the almond essence very thoroughly.

7 Decorate with the whipped cream, toasted almonds and freshly picked mint leaves.

PHOTOGRAPHS:

Chequered Salad; Herb Salad; Tomato and Oatmeal Tart
Demerara Meringues with a Fruit Sauce; Cream Curd Tarts and Strawberries;
Elderflower and Gooseberry Cream
Turbot baked in a Sage Sauce

LOGANBERRY ICE CREAM

Loganberries are one of our favourite fruits. Like mulberries, they should not be picked until they are almost black. A truly ripe loganberry has a vibrant, singing clarity of taste ideally suited to ice cream, which can lose character when frozen. Blackcurrants and damsons also have this strength.

This is the simplest form of ice cream, made with just sweetened fruit purée and cream. It may set a little harder than ice cream made with a custard base, so take it out of the freezer 20 minutes before serving in normal conditions. Ice cream made with soft fruits also tends to crystallize, and unless you have an ice cream maker, it is necessary to break up the crystals – I usually beat the mixture in the food processor or electric mixer halfway through freezing.

SERVES: 6
PREPARATION TIME: 15 minutes
FREEZING TIME: approximately 4 hours

680g (1½ lb) fresh loganberries
225g (½ lb) light muscovado sugar
285ml (½ pint) fresh double cream

1 Push the loganberries through a plastic sieve into a bowl. Sweeten the purée and set aside 120ml (4 fl oz) for the sauce.
2 Whip the cream lightly and add the larger quantity of loganberry purée.
3 If you are using an ice cream maker, follow the manufacturer's instructions. If making the ice cream by hand, put into either a plastic container with a lid or a stainless steel tin covered with foil and freeze.
4 After 3 hours, remove the ice cream from the freezer and beat thoroughly. Return to the container and freeze until firm.
5 Twenty minutes before serving, remove from the freezer to allow the ice cream to soften. You can also put in the refrigerator 1 hour before serving.
6 Serve three medium scoops in a wine glass and spoon a little of the dark coloured sauce over the paler ice cream.

SUMMER MENUS

SIMPLE SUPPER

Cucumber and Fennel Soup (page 58)

Rice Salad (page 77)

Loganberry Ice Cream (page 98)

VEGETARIAN SUPPER OR LIGHT LUNCH

Lettuce and Pea Soufflé (page 62)

Stuffed Peppers (page 80)
Herb Salad (page 89)

Great Granny's Velvet Cream with Fresh Raspberries (page 93)

DINNER PARTY

Beetroot Soup (page 55)

Callaminco with Apple and Horseradish Sauce (page 61)

Turbot Baked in a Sage Sauce (page 71)

Courgettes with Rosemary (page 73)
Garden Peas
Steamed New Potatoes with Chives

Lettuce and Grapefruit Salad (page 87)

Cream Curd Hearts with Mixed Soft Fruits (page 95)
Demerara Meringues with Bitter Chocolate Sauce (page 92)

Autumn

How elegantly Keats has captured the spirit of autumn. Languorous after the heat and toil of summer, the voluptuous and sensual pleasure of autumn almost overwhelms one. Now there is much work for the wheelbarrow, ferrying produce from garden to kitchen and store room. Strings of golden onions, violet shallots and silvery garlic, knobbly jade green or amber pumpkins and the heavenly scent of the apple room delight us again.

There is infinite enjoyment in the sight of so much variety in colour and shape and in the scents of the ripening fruits. Part of me wants to devour these goodies all now, whilst the more prudent squirrel in me compels me to put aside time for preserving and preparation for storage. Soft fruits can go straight from the gathering basket to the freezer. Quinces must be laid up carefully to ripen. Mulberries, in shorter supply and painstaking to pick, appear on the table immediately as jelly, ice cream and sauces.

Tomatoes starting in July but at last ripening prolifically are used constantly now, but any surplus are frozen just as they are, for those wonderful sauces and stews to come later. It simply is not possible to buy commercial tomatoes in or out of season to compare with the taste of a homegrown variety such as Ailsa Craig or Gardener's Delight.

With autumn comes the time for wild fruits such as blackberries, sloes, rosehips and elderberries, mushrooms and edible fungi, and game like duck, venison, pheasant and pike. Time to reflect on the fruitfulness of summer and to look forward to the comforts of winter.

LOVAGE SOUP

There are still fresh new leaves of lovage, if you delve inside the plant which has flowered and regrown before the foliage dies in the first frost.

SERVES: 6
PREPARATION TIME: minimal
COOKING TIME: 15–20 minutes

55g (2 oz) unsalted butter
1 medium-sized onion, chopped
1 medium-sized potato, peeled and chopped
handful of fresh lovage leaves
1.1 litres (2 pints) hot ham stock
sea salt
freshly ground black pepper
2 egg yolks (optional)
wholemeal croûtons to garnish
bacon fat to fry

1 Melt the butter in a large saucepan over a moderate heat. Add the onion and potato and cook for 5 minutes.
2 Add the lovage leaves. When they have wilted, pour on the ham stock, bring to the boil and simmer until the potato is soft, about 10 minutes. Remove from the heat.
3 Liquidize and sieve. Season to taste, reheat and serve with wholemeal croûtons that have been fried in bacon fat.

For richer soup, whisk 2 egg yolks and stir them into the soup after it has been liquidized, but do not allow the soup to boil when you are reheating it.

TOMATO AND ROSEMARY SOUP

The rich tasting tomatoes of Autumn make a lovely soup combined with aromatic rosemary.

SERVES: 6
PREPARATION TIME: minimal
COOKING TIME: 30 minutes

30g (1 oz) unsalted butter
1 medium-sized onion, sliced
570ml (1 pint) hot chicken stock
900g (2 lb) ripe tomatoes
3 tablespoonsful water
sprig of fresh rosemary
sea salt
freshly ground black pepper

1 Melt the butter in a large saucepan over a moderate heat and cook the onion until it is transparent, about 5 minutes. Add the chicken stock and cook for a further 10 minutes. Liquidize and sieve.
2 Meanwhile, chop the tomatoes and put in another saucepan with water. Cook until soft, about 15–20 minutes. Remove from the heat, push through a sieve and stir the tomato purée into the stock. Simmer with the rosemary for 10 minutes. Season and serve hot, garnished with a grinding of black pepper.

PUMPKINS

Golden pumpkins basking in the sun, bursting with ripeness, seem the very quintessence of the abundance of Autumn. They impart a wonderful velvety texture to soups and their vivid colour enlivens pies, tarts and preserves. Their slightly earthy flavour responds to the strong, vibrant tastes of tomatoes, herbs and spices.

Some varieties, such as Buttercup, are stunning cooked as a vegetable, diced and served with lemon butter. They have a surprisingly satisfactory mealy texture and fragrant taste.

PUMPKIN AND SAFFRON SOUP

A mellow, golden, velvety soup, most delicious of all made with wild duck stock, but any good meaty stock will do.

SERVES: 6
PREPARATION TIME: 20 minutes
COOKING TIME: 30 minutes

900g (2 lb) Buttercup pumpkin
55g (2 oz) unsalted butter
1 medium-sized onion
1.4 litres (2½ pints) hot wild duck stock
few strands saffron, soaked in a little cold water
sea salt
freshly ground black pepper
wholemeal croûtons to garnish
bacon fat to fry

1 Peel, deseed and chop the pumpkin into 2.5cm (1-inch) dice.
2 Put the butter in a large saucepan and sweat the onion for a few minutes, add the pumpkin and cook for a further few minutes.
3 Heat the stock to boiling point and pour over the vegetables. Add the saffron and simmer until the pumpkin is soft. Remove from the heat, whizz in a liquidizer and sieve if you want a really smooth soup.
4 Serve piping hot, with wholemeal croûtons crisply fried in bacon fat.

PIED PIPER SOUP

A simple recipe can still reveal a dramatic effect, as in this two-tone, scarlet and gold soup.

SERVES: 6
PREPARATION TIME: 20 minutes
COOKING TIME: 45 minutes

30g (1 oz) unsalted butter
900g (2 lb) Buttercup pumpkin
1 medium-sized onion, roughly chopped
1.1 litres (2 pints) hot chicken stock
455g (1 lb) ripe tomatoes
3 tablespoonsful water
2 cloves garlic
1 bay leaf
sea salt
freshly ground black pepper

1 Peel, deseed and chop the pumpkin into large dice.
2 Melt the butter in a large saucepan, add the pumpkin and onion and cook over a moderate heat without browning for 10 minutes. Add the chicken stock and continue cooking until the vegetables are soft. Remove from the heat, whizz in a liquidizer and sieve. Season and return to a clean saucepan.
3 Put the tomatoes in another saucepan with the water, garlic and bay leaf and cook over a moderate heat for 10 minutes. Remove from the heat and sieve into a clean saucepan. Season to taste.
4 When ready to serve, reheat both soups separately. Have hot soup bowls or plates ready. Half-fill the bowls with the golden pumpkin soup, then ladle the scarlet tomato purée into the centre of the bowl. Or, divide the bowls or soup plates with a piece of card – cut to size – and fill one side with red soup and the other with yellow. Carefully lift out the card. The colours should remain distinct. Fresh milled black pepper is all that is needed as a garnish.

APPLES AND HOPE END

When my grandfather bought the Hope End estate in 1947, his intention, strangely enough, was to turn the derelict ruin of a house, covered with creepers and hemmed in by a tangle of trees, into a hotel. Preliminary work was started, but after he died, my father decided to put the building to use as a refrigerated fruit store. Every Autumn the house was loaded with boxes of apples; their perfume filled the storage chambers, machinery hummed and one end of the house became the busy packing department.

Some of the apples my father grew had names like Beauty of Bath, Lord Lambourne and Egremont Russet, but my favourite was the local Worcester Pearmain. Picked at their peak, they were the reddest-skinned, whitest-fleshed, juiciest, crispest and sweetest apples I have ever tasted.

We have planted several other local apples in our garden: Pitmarston Pineapple from Worcester — tiny, nuggetty and golden-fleshed with an exquisite flavour; King's Acre Pippin from Hereford — large, rough-skinned, rosy-red with a deliciously sharp, yet sweet flavour, long-keeping and ideally suited to our climate, and Ashmead from Gloucester — another robust and hardy apple.

CIDER AND PERRY

Every Spring the apple and pear blossom drifted up the valleys and over the hills of the West Country. The orchards of cider apples and perry pears, inhabited by large and venerable trees, were an integral part of the farming economy.

Every Autumn on each farm and smallholding, the hard, tart little cider apples and pears were beaten and shaken from the trees and carted to the mills and presses. The fruit was first crushed in the circular stone mill, hand-hewn from local stone. Then the pulp was transferred to the press and the juices strained through layers of hessian into barrels where it was left to ferment. The resultant scrumpy was often notoriously powerful and rough, but the farm workers received measures of cider and perry as part of their pay — vital to them through the hard days of the winter and the toils of harvest time. It was also thought to be safer to drink than the water, which was often polluted.

Now, sadly, more of the old orchards are grubbed out every year and the cider mills stand unused and mossy, filled with garden flowers. A few orchards are being planted again by enterprising, young cider makers and stainless steel equipment and some measure of technology has taken the guesswork out of the process.

It is still possible to buy the old varieties of perry pears. We have planted Barland and Moorcroft, which originated a few fields away from Hope End, to help keep tradition alive.

Elizabeth Barrett Browning describes the apple orchards at Hope End in her poem,
'The Lost Bower'.

'Gentle the land is, where my daily
Steps in jocund childhood played.
Dimpled close with hill and valley.
Dappled very close with shade.
Summer snow of apple blossom running up from glade to glade.'

HALIBUT IN SPICED PERRY SAUCE

Halibut has the most wonderful pearly-white, firm-textured flesh. We feel very lucky when a good piece comes our way. It makes our trip to the market really worthwhile.

SERVES: 6
PREPARATION TIME: minimal
BAKING TIME: 15 minutes
COOKING TIME: 10 minutes

unsalted butter to grease
6 fresh halibut fillets (about 115–140g (4–5 oz) each)
270ml (½ pint) perry
120ml (4 fl oz) fresh double cream
I teaspoonful ground cumin
seeds of 6 cardamom pods, crushed with a pestle
and mortar
I teaspoonful freshly grated root ginger
squeeze of lemon juice
sea salt
freshly ground black pepper
fresh flat-leaved parsley to garnish

1 Preheat the oven to 375°F/190°C/Gas mark 5.

2 Butter a baking dish, arrange the halibut fillets in it, add the perry and bake for 15 minutes. Remove from the oven.

3 Pour off most of the cooking liquor into a wide frying pan. Keep the fish warm and covered while preparing the sauce. Quickly reduce the cooking liquor over a high heat until about 2 teaspoonsful are left. Reduce the heat, stir in cream, cumin and cardamom seeds and allow to bubble and thicken. Add lemon juice and seasoning to taste.

4 To serve, pour the sauce around the fillets and finish with sprigs of flat-leaved parsley.

PIKE WITH CHIVE MAYONNAISE

A jack (young pike) is ideal for this light starter. I buy my pike gutted, but with the head and tail still on as I think the fish stays fresher this way. Watercress, or even parsley, can be substituted for the chives to colour and flavour the mayonnaise.

SERVES: 6 as a starter
PREPARATION TIME: 20 minutes
BAKING TIME: 30 minutes

1.1–1.4kg (2½–3 lb) jack pike
1 bay leaf
fresh parsley stalks
285ml (½ pint) dry white wine

CHIVE MAYONNAISE

2 egg yolks
2 tablespoonsful cider vinegar or lemon juice
1 small clove garlic
140ml (¼ pint) cold pressed olive oil
140ml (¼ pint) sunflower oil
pinch of sea salt
2 tablespoonsful chopped fresh chives

1 Preheat the oven to 375°F/190°C/Gas mark 5.

2 Cut the head and tail off the pike, lay it on a sheet of aluminium foil in a roasting pan, tuck the bay leaf and parsley in the body cavity and pour the wine over it. Seal the parcel and bake for about 30 minutes, or until cooked through. Remove from the oven and allow to cool.

3 It is then easy to detach the leathery skin and fillet the pike. Divide the fish into 6 portions. You will find that most of the bones can be pulled out from the ends of the sections.

4 Make the mayonnaise in a food processor or liquidizer, adding the chives during the last second or two.

5 To serve, spoon a little mayonnaise attractively over or beside each portion of fish and strew with a few more chopped chives.

HADDOCK AND MUSSEL
HOT POTS WITH LANGOUSTINES

There should be no problem finding good haddock and succulent mussels as long as the weather is clement at sea. Whole langoustines or Dublin Bay prawns are a small, dramatic flourish for this dish of many colours, white saffron, pink, orange and indigo.

SERVES: 6 as a starter or 4 as a supper dish
PREPARATION TIME: 30 minutes
COOKING TIME: 20 minutes
BAKING TIME: 15–20 minutes

3-4 dozen mussels in their shells
140ml (¼ pint) dry white wine
6 whole cooked langoustines
455g (1 lb) fresh haddock, skinned and filleted

SAUCE

45g (1½ oz) unsalted butter	1 teaspoonful aniseed
3 shallots, chopped	1 tablespoon made English mustard
120ml (4 fl oz) water	sea salt
120ml (4 fl oz) dry vermouth or dry white wine	freshly ground black pepper
30g (1 oz) wholemeal flour	3 tablespoonsful wholemeal breadcrumbs
140ml (¼ pint) mussel cooking liquor	wholemeal bread and butter to serve
140ml (¼ pint) fresh double cream	

1 Put the mussels into a bowl of cold water, discarding any that float or do not close up tight when tapped with a knife. Scrub the mussels and take off the beards.
2 Tip the mussels into a heavy casserole with the wine and cook them quickly over a high heat until they open. As they do, lift them out with kitchen tongs into a colander on a plate. It is important not to overcook and toughen them. Discard any mussels that remain closed. Strain off and reserve the cooking liquid left in the casserole and on the plate through a very fine mesh sieve and reserve.
3 Extract the mussels, keeping 6 of the most attractive shells.
4 If the langoustines are raw, plunge them into boiling water. They will be cooked when the water reaches boiling point again. Remove from the heat and drain.
5 Make the sauce. Melt l tablespoonful of the butter in a saucepan, add the shallots and water

and sizzle until the shallots are soft. Add the vermouth and reduce to a syrup.

6 Mash the remaining butter and flour with a fork. Over a moderate heat, add the mussel cooling liquor and the cream to the shallots and whisk in small knobs of the butter-flour mixture to thicken the sauce. Remove from the heat.

7 Crush the aniseed with a pestle and mortar to release the aroma and stir into the sauce with the mustard. Season to taste.

8 Preheat the oven to 375°F/190°C/Gas mark 5. Flake the haddock and arrange in 6 shallow ovenproof dishes interspersed with the mussels and a mussel shell on either side. Ladle over the sauce, scatter with breadcrumbs and bake for 15–20 minutes. Five minutes before serving, place a pink langoustine on top of each dish in the oven to heat through.

9 Serve hot with wholemeal bread and butter to mop up the juices.

I keep the mussels in a bowl of cold water in the refrigerator with a handful of oatmeal added to keep them fresh and clean until I am ready to use them.

NAVARIN OF AUTUMN VEGETABLES

I often cook an Autumn navarin using swedes, instead of the young turnips of Spring, and the last of the good peas and carrots. This is a simple vegetarian version of the navarin of lamb and a delicious way of showing off all the lovely vegetables in the garden at this time of year. You can substitute other fresh vegetables if you wish.

SERVES: 6
PREPARATION TIME: 10 minutes
COOKING TIME: 15 minutes
BAKING TIME: 45 minutes

SAUCE

55g (2 oz) unsalted butter	115g (4 oz) fresh carrots, scraped and cut into
55g (2 oz) wholemeal flour	'little finger' lengths
570ml (1 pint) ripe tomatoes, cooked, sieved	115g (4 oz) small onions, peeled
and puréed	340g (¾ lb) fresh broad beans, podded or 115g
6 cloves garlic, chopped	(4 oz) runner beans, cut into 2.5cm (1-inch) lengths
bouquet garni	225g (½ lb) fresh garden peas
sea salt	55g (2 oz) unsalted butter
freshly ground black pepper	225g (½ lb) fresh mushrooms
115g (4 oz) fresh swedes, peeled and cut into	squeeze of lemon juice
1.25cm (½-inch) dice	chopped fresh English parsley to garnish

1 Make the sauce. Melt the butter in a heavy casserole over a moderate heat. Stir in the flour and cook for 1 minute. Add the cider and cook until thickened. Stir in the tomato purée, garlic, bouquet garni and seasoning. Mix together well.

2 Preheat the oven to 300°F/150°C/Gas mark 2. Add the swedes, carrots and onions to the casserole, bring to simmering point, then transfer to the oven, cover and bake for 45 minutes, adding the broad or runner beans after 25 minutes and the peas after 35 minutes.

3 About 5 minutes before the casserole is ready, melt the butter in a frying pan over a moderate heat and cook the mushrooms quickly, adding a squeeze of lemon juice.

4 Remove the casserole from the oven, testing the vegetables to make quite sure they are cooked. Lastly, add the mushrooms with their cooking liquid.

5 Sprinkle with fresh chopped parsley and serve.

DILL PORK

This recipe originates in Scandinavia. Traces of dill and coriander were found in the Viking remains at York. The dill sauce is also delicious with fish (see Pike Dumplings, page 158), drawing its power and depth from the ripe tomatoes and another layer of intensity from the aromatic dill.

It is difficult to find really good pork. Gone are the days when every cottager depended on his pig to feed his family through the winter. However, traditionally reared pork is beginning to be available again and is worth seeking out for its refined texture, better flavour and purity.

SERVES: 6
PREPARATION TIME: 20 minutes
COOKING TIME: 15 minutes
BAKING TIME: 1 hour

900g (2 lb) traditionally-reared pork tenderloin

STUFFING

55g (2 oz) wholemeal breadcrumbs

1 tablespoonful dill seeds (whizzed in the liquidizer to release their aroma)

1 tablespoonful tomato purée

juice of ½ lemon

freshly ground black pepper

2 tablespoonsful cold pressed olive oil to brown meat

DILL SAUCE

85g (3 oz) shallots, chopped

680g (1½ lb) tomatoes, cooked and sieved

3 tablespoonsful chopped fresh dillweed or 1 tablespoonful dill seeds, whizzed as above

2 teaspoonsful cornflour (optional)

1 bay leaf

sea salt

120ml (4 fl oz) fresh soured cream (optional)

fresh dillweed or garnish

1 Cut the pork tenderloin in half horizontally, then into 12.5cm (5-inch) lengths.

Place a piece of cling film over them and beat the pork out thinly with a rolling pin.

2 Mix the stuffing ingredients together well and spread a portion over each fillet. Roll up and secure with a cocktail stick, trimming the ends if they are too ragged.

3 Heat the oil in a frying pan, brown the pork rolls, then fit then into a heavy casserole.

4 Preheat the oven to 300°F/150°C/Gas mark 2. Make the sauce. Cook the shallots gently in the olive oil for 10 minutes, then add the cooked tomato purée. If the sauce seems too thin, mix in the cornflour, mixed with a little tomato to a paste and cook until thickened. Stir in the fresh chopped dill weed or dill seeds, bay leaf and salt to taste. Pour the sauce over the pork in the casserole, cover and bake for 1 hour.

5 Just before serving, stir in the soured cream, if using, and decorate with fresh dill fronds.

LEMON LAMB

This is a spicy lamb recipe from North Africa and a complete contrast to a traditional roast. The marinade tenderizes the lamb and allows the spices to impregnate the meat. English lamb is beautifully tender, so I have cut down on the usual time for steeping the meat in the marinade, but the lamb still benefits from the absorption of flavours.

SERVES: 6
PREPARATION TIME: 10 minutes
MARINATING TIME: 2 hours
COOKING TIME: 10–20 minutes
BAKING TIME: 1 hour

1.4kg (3 lb) boned leg of lamb	hot chicken stock
4 tablespoonsful olive oil	225g (½ lb) fresh mushrooms, sliced
6 cloves garlic, finely chopped	sea salt
2 lemons, well scrubbed	freshly ground black pepper
1 teaspoonsful ground coriander	fresh root ginger to garnish (optional)
½ teaspoonful ground ginger	4 lemon twists
2 medium-sized onions, finely sliced	fresh flat-leaved parsley to garnish
2 tablespoonsful wholemeal flour	brown rice and toasted, flaked almonds to serve

1 Cut the lamb into 2.5cm (1-inch) cubes. Put into a bowl with the oil, garlic, the rind of 1 lemon, cumin, coriander and ginger and marinate for about 2 hours, turning the mixture quite often.

2 Remove the lamb with a slotted spoon, reserving the marinade and brown the lamb on all sides in a heavy saucepan or casserole. Add the reserved marinade, the onions and scatter with the flour. Brown for a further moment or two and pour on enough chicken stock to cover. Bring to simmering point over a moderate heat. Remove from the heat.

3 Preheat the oven to 300°F/150°C/Gas mark 2. Make a tight seal for the lamb by putting a sheet of aluminium foil over the pan and cover with the lid. Bake for about 1 hour, or until the lamb is tender, adding the mushrooms after 40 minutes. Remove from the oven.

4 If the meat and mushroom juices have made the sauce too thin, remove the meat, keeping it warm, and reduce the sauce by fast boiling. Stir constantly, as the small amount of flour used will catch if it can. Strain through a fine sieve. Add lemon juice to taste. Season with salt and pepper. Embellish with lemon twists, very fine shavings of peeled ginger root if liked, and flat-leave parsley. Serve with brown rice and toasted flaked almonds.

Beef in Mustard and Savory Sauce

The savory in the title of this recipe is the herb winter savory. Having discovered for myself how beautifully it goes with beef, I was amused to find a recipe using this combination in an old Herefordshire cookery book. Winter savory does get a little coarse if the weather is harsh and needs to be chopped very finely. The rump steak should be really well-hung. Just keeping it in the refrigerator, covered with greaseproof paper, for a couple of days seems to help.

SERVES: 6
PREPARATION TIME: minimal
COOKING TIME: 10–15 minutes

900g (2 lb) well-hung rump steak
1 tablespoonful cold pressed olive oil
180ml (6 fl oz) fresh double cream
2 tablespoonsful English mustard made up with water
3 teaspoonsful cider vinegar
1 tablespoonful finely chopped fresh winter savory
few whole sprigs fresh winter savory to garnish

1 Cut the steak into small strips.
2 Heat the oil in a heavy frying pan over a medium-high heat. Add the steak and sear, reduce the heat and cook briefly. Remove from the pan with a slotted spoon.
3 Keep the meat warm and covered while you make the sauce.
4 Add the cream, mustard, vinegar and chopped savory to the pan and reduce the sauce to a coating consistency. Turn the meat over in the sauce and heat through.
5 Serve, spiked with tiny savory sprigs.

MARROW WITH GINGER BUTTER

Vegetable marrows are often derided as watery and tasteless. The monster marrows portrayed in comic strips and seaside postcards would be, but a juicy, young marrow, fed on rich compost and picked when it is no larger than a foot long, cooks to a vivid, translucent green and has a lovely freshness to it. The ginger butter gives it some punch. Served this way, it is equally delicious with roast beef or roast chicken. Pumpkins, which have a much fuller flavour, are best presented as vegetables diced and steamed and then dressed with lemon butter, or fried in a little olive oil and sprinkled with parsley which cuts through their mealy richness.

SERVES: 6
PREPARATION TIME: 10 minutes
COOKING TIME: 20 minutes

900g (2 lb) young marrows
85g (3 oz) unsalted butter
½ teaspoonful ground ginger, or to taste or
grated fresh root ginger to taste
sea salt
freshly ground black pepper
fresh flat-leaved parsley to garnish

1 Cut the rind off the marrow, deseed and cut into 2cm (¾-inch) dice.
2 Cook in a steamer until tender, about 20 minutes, but do not allow to go mushy. Transfer to a warm serving dish.
3 Barely melt the butter, then remove from the heat. Stir in the ground or fresh ginger and season with salt and pepper. Dribble the fragrant butter over the marrow and garnish with flat-leaved parsley.

CAULIFLOWER AND SAGE

This is an alternative light and savoury dressing for cauliflower.

SERVES: 6
PREPARATION TIME: minimal
COOKING TIME: 12–15 minutes

I medium-sized cauliflower
I teaspoonful cornflour
140ml (¼ pint) natural yogurt
sea salt
freshly ground black pepper
I tablespoonful chopped fresh sage
whole sage leaves and/or sage flowers to garnish

1 Trim the outer leaves of the cauliflower, cut into 2.5cm (1-inch) florets and cook, including any of the fresh inner green leaves, until a sharp knife will just piece the stalk, about 5–8 minutes. Remove from the heat and keep warm.

2 Meanwhile, make the sauce. Mix the cornflour with a little yogurt. Heat the remaining yogurt in a saucepan over a low heat, then beat it into the paste, stirring hard. Return the mixture to the pan and stir until the sauce thickens. Cook for 2 minutes. (Yogurt becomes too slack when heated unless it is stabilized with cornflour.) Remove from the heat and stir in the chopped sage.

3 Pour the sauce over the cauliflower and serve, garnished with sage leaves and flowers.

Another good, and even lighter, sauce for cauliflower is a trickle of melted butter, sprinkled with toasted sesame seeds.

CELERY AND GRAPE SALAD

The celebrated Waldorf Salad is an established favourite. As a mid-meal salad. I use French dressing made with walnut oil, but as an accompaniment to a cold table or when serving with baked potatoes as a light supper dish, creamy yogurt is a lighter echo of the original mayonnaise dressing. It is splendid served with cold meats, such as turkey leftovers after Christmas.

Serves: 6
Preparation time: 15 minutes

I head of celery
170g (6 oz) grapes, preferably black
2–3 dessert apples (Cox's or a Russet variety)
85g (3 oz) shelled walnuts
watercress to garnish

DRESSING

5 tablespoonsful walnut oil
I teaspoonful cider vinegar
sea salt
freshly ground black pepper
or 6 tablespoonsful thick natural yogurt

1 Cut the celery crossways into small, neat slices, including all the fresh green leaves. Halve the grapes and remove the pips.
2 Just before serving, core and slice the apples, leaving the skin on and cut into 1.25cm (½-inch) dice.
3 Toss all the ingredients in the chosen dressing and snip some watercress over the top.

APPLE AND FENNEL SALAD

For this salad, try to find an aniseedy or fresh-tasting apple, such as Ellison's Orange or a crimson-coloured one like Belle de Boskoop to point up the emerald of the fennel fronds. This salad is delicious either served on its own, or complementing cold pork, chicken or pâté.

Serves: 6
Preparation time: 20 minutes

2 Florence fennel bulbs
4 dessert apples

DRESSING

1 clove garlic
large pinch of sea salt
1 teaspoonful fennel seeds
5 teaspoonsful virgin olive oil
1 teaspoonful cider vinegar
1 teaspoonful Meaux mustard

1 First make the dressing. Crush the garlic with the salt. Whizz the fennel seeds in the liquidizer to release their aroma, then add the garlic and the remaining ingredients and whizz together.

2 Cut the fennel bulbs in half lengthways, then cut across in thin slices. Depending on how much fennel frond there is, either mix into the salad or reserve for decoration. Leaving the pretty peel on the apples, cut, core and then slice them to match the fennel pieces.

3 Dress the salad, tossing well, to prevent the apples from browning.

MULBERRY AND MELON

This dessert is almost as dramatic to look at as it is to taste. In a hot year Ogen melons ripen lusciously in the greenhouse with attentive watering.

SERVES: 6

PREPARATION TIME: 10 minutes

3 ripe Ogen melons
455g (1 lb) well ripened mulberries
golden granulated sugar to taste
arrowroot (optional)
180ml (6 fl oz) double cream

1 Cut the melons in half and scoop out the seeds.

2 Whizz the mulberries in the liquidizer, sieve well and sweeten. Mulberry juice tends to be watery. If this worries you stiffen it with a little arrowroot – about 1 teaspoonful to 150ml (¼ pint) liquid, warmed just enough to thicken.

3 Fill the melon hollows almost to the brim and pipe a circlet of whipped cream round the edge.

MULBERRY AND APPLE PIE

The taste of mulberry is a surprise: unusual, dry and lingering like a good wine. You only need a few fruits to make an impression but they must be nearly black to have a perfectly developed flavour. The trees do take about ten years to crop if you are starting from scratch – so plant one now or seek out an old, established tree and beg some fruit at the end of September from the lucky owners. Be sure to wear old clothes as mulberry juice seems to spatter everywhere.

I have noticed there is no need to glaze this pastry. In fact, if wholemeal pastry is glazed with milk or egg it usually catches and overbrowns. It turns a beautiful colour without any aid.

SERVES: 6
PREPARATION TIME: preparing the pastry,
plus 15 minutes baking
COOKING TIME: 10–15 minutes
BAKING TIME: 20 minutes

395g (14 oz) Wholemeal Puff Pastry (page 177)

FILLING

680g (1½ lb) apples, such as Howgate Wonder

120ml (4 fl oz) fresh apple juice

3 whole cloves

225g (½ lb) fresh mulberries

3–4 tablespoonsful unrefined light muscovado sugar

1 Make the pastry and leave to rest.
2 Peel, slice and core the apples and cook to a pulp in the apple juice with cloves. Soften the mulberries in a small pan over a low heat until the juices start to run.
3 Stir into the apple and sweeten to taste. Tip into a 1 litre (2 pint) dish with a broad rim. Allow to cool.
4 Damp the rim of the dish and cover with the pastry. Cut two slits in the top to allow the steam to escape and decorate with leaves and flowers from the pastry trimmings.
5 Bake at 425°F/220°C/Gas mark 7 for about twenty minutes till the pastry has cooked and turned a lovely brown. Serve hot or cold with thick golden Jersey cream.

APPLE AND CALVADOS TART

The history of English cooking is inevitably entwined with France. This tart shows the intermingling of influences. The French do not have 'cooking apples', but use instead dessert apples such as Belle de Boskoop which we grow and consider one of our best. The filling is pure essence of apple, intensified by Calvados and the pastry is sweet and nutty.

SERVES: 8–10
PREPARATION TIME: preparing and baking the
pastry case, plus 20 minutes
COOKING TIME: 10 minutes
BAKING TIME: 20 minutes

HAZELNUT SHORTCRUST PASTRY

55g (2 oz) wholemeal flour
30g (1 oz) lightly toasted hazelnuts, ground
45g (1½ oz) cold unsalted butter
1 teaspoonful fine demerara sugar (page 92)
3 tablespoonsful beaten egg

FILLING

455g (1 lb) Bramley apples
juice 1 lemon
2–3 tablespoonsful light muscovado sugar
2 tablespoonsful Calvados
455g (1 lb) Belle de Boskoop or other red-skinned dessert apples
fine demerara sugar
2 tablespoonsful redcurrant jelly, melted

CINNAMON CREAM

140ml (½ pint) fresh double cream
1 teaspoonful fine demerara sugar
½ teaspoonful ground cinnamon

1 Make the pastry according to the method on page 176 adding the hazelnuts at the 'bread-crumb' stage. Leave to rest at least 20 minutes, then use to line a 22.5cm (9-inch) flan tin with a removable base and bake blind. Set aside to cool.

2 Peel, core and slice the Bramley apples and cook them over a low heat with half the lemon juice, stirring to prevent the apples from burning. Stir in the sugar until it has dissolved, add the Calvados and tip the thick pulp into the prepared pastry case.

3 Preheat the oven to 400°F/200°C/Gas mark 6. Cut, core and slice the unpeeled dessert apples, and arrange in concentric circles on top of the apple purée overlapping slightly, brushing with the remaining lemon juice from time to time. Glaze with melted redcurrant jelly. Sift a little sugar over the top.

4 Bake for 20 minutes or until the apples start to brown.

5 Meanwhile, make the Cinnamon Cream by whipping together all the ingredients until firm.

6 Serve hot or cold with dollops of Cinnamon Cream.

APPLE DUMPLINGS WITH BLACKBERRIES

Jane Austen and Queen Victoria both had a penchant for baked apples. For apple dumplings —
a lustier version encased in pastry — choose even-sized apples and score a line round the tops
to prevent them from bursting open as they bake. Dessert apples, such as Ellison's Orange, are
lovely for this dish.

SERVES: 6

PREPARATION TIME: making the pastry,
plus 40 minutes

BAKING TIME: 30–40 minutes

COOKING TIME: 5 minutes

PASTRY

225g (8 oz) wholemeal flour
30g (1 oz) unrefined fine demerara sugar
finely grated rind of 1 lemon
55g (2 oz) cold unsalted butter
55g (2 oz) lard
8 tablespoonful iced water

FILLING

6 medium-sized dessert apples
455g (1 lb) fresh wild blackberries
85g (3 oz) unrefined muscovado sugar
butter to grease
6-8 tablespoonful honey to glaze
120ml (4 fl oz) cider
hot custard sauce (page 187) or fresh thick Jersey cream
to serve

1 Make the pastry in the usual manner (page 176) and leave to rest, wrapped in a floured
plastic bag in a cool place while preparing the filling.

2 Core the apples and score a line about 2cm (¾-inch) from the tops with the tip of a sharp
knife.

3 Divide the pastry into 6 portions and roll out into 8-inch circles. Preheat the oven to
400°F/200°C/Gas mark 6.

4 Place an apple in the centre of each pastry circle. Fill the cavities with blackberries

(reserving those left over for the sauce) and top with the sugar. Fold the pastry up around the apples, not too tightly, and damp the edges to secure at the top, leaving a small opening for the steam to escape. Make decorative leaves with the pastry trimmings and press one or two on top of each apple. Arrange on a well-buttered metal (preferably stainless steel) baking dish and glaze with the honey.

5 Bake for 30–40 minutes. If the apples, during their baking time, appear to be splitting open their pastry jackets, reduce the heat and bake a little longer. Remove from the oven and place the dumplings on a warm plate.

6 Deglaze the honey and sugar syrup left in the baking dish with the cider on top of the stove. Add the remaining blackberries and heat through for a moment, then remove from the heat and purée the sauce in a blender. Sieve and sweeten if necessary.

7 Pour the blackberry sauce round the apples and serve either with hot custard sauce or thick Jersey cream handed round separately.

CHERRY AND RICE BRÛLÉE

Morello cherries, those useful denizens of north walls, sharpen up a creamy rice under a brittle, caramelized crust in this version of a creme brûlée which can sometimes be a little too rich after a good meal. I often use a strong-tasting fruit, such as gooseberries, raspberries, Blaisdon plums (a local variety), or blackcurrants under a cap of custard as an equally effective contrast. Rice is easily elevated into special, even grand dishes with the enrichment of cream and eggs and the addition of preserved and glacéed fruits and spices.

SERVES: 6
SOAKING TIME: overnight (optional)
COOKING TIME: 10 minutes
BAKING TIME: 2 hours
CHILLING TIME: 1–2 hours
GRILLING TIME: approximately 5 minutes

140ml (¼ pint) boiling water
55g (2 oz) short-grain brown rice
570ml (1 pint) fresh milk or half milk and half single cream
1 tablespoonful unrefined light muscovado sugar or
1 tablespoonful honey
vanilla pod
30g (1 oz) unsalted butter
freshly grated nutmeg
225g (½ lb) fresh Morello cherries
sugar to taste
6 tablespoonsful unrefined fine demerara sugar (page 92)

1 Wash the rice in a colander under a cold tap to remove excess starch. Drain well.
2 Put the rice into a saucepan with the water and boil for 5 minutes to start the rice swelling; alternatively, soak in the milk overnight.
3 Put the rice, milk, sugar or honey and vanilla pod into a baking dish, dab with the butter and grate some nutmeg over the top. Bake at 325°F/170°C/Gas mark 3 for 2 hours, by which time the grains of rice should be plump and creamy.
4 Cook the cherries gently over a low heat until the juice runs. Remove from the heat and stone if you wish. Sweeten to taste and mix into the rice. Spoon portions of the mixture into 6 fireproof ramekins and put into the refrigerator to firm up for 1–2 hours.
5 Just before serving, smooth 1 tablespoonful demerara sugar over the top of each ramekin

and grill under a high heat until the sugar melts and caramelizes, forming a brittle, glossy coating over the surface. (It is difficult to give more precise directions as everyone's grill is different and I find that each time I make a brûlée the sugar behaves differently, but it is always delicious to eat.)

6 Serve fairly soon after grilling as the sugar will begin to absorb moisture from the atmosphere. So keep away from steaming pots!

PHOTOGRAPHS:

Pumpkin and Saffron Soup
Navarin of Autumn Vegetables
Lemon Lamb; Cherry and Rice Brulee
Chestnut and Pear Flan

BARLEY KERNEL PUDDING

This is one of our family's favourite milk puddings. I like to cook it quickly, using the porridge method to keep the shape and feel of the grains. The barley kernels cook to a most satisfying texture and are a fine foil for stewed or fresh fruit, or simply served in the old-fashioned way with a good blob of strong red jam.

SERVES: 6
COOKING TIME: approximately 30 minutes
SETTING TIME: (optional) 2 hours

60g (2¼ oz) barley kernels
30g (I oz) sultanas
1–2 tablespoonsful unrefined golden granulated sugar
850ml (I½ pints) fresh milk
I vanilla pod or cinnamon stick or ground seeds of 6 cardamom pods
fresh double cream (optional)
fresh or stewed fruit or jam

1 Put the barley kernels, sultanas, sugar and chosen flavouring into a heavy-based saucepan. Add the milk gradually, over a low heat, stirring well with a wooden spoon until the kernels have absorbed the milk, softened and reached the consistency of a moderately thick porridge, about 30 minutes. Remove from the heat and stir in some cream for an extra-rich pudding if desired.
2 Serve hot and cold with fresh or stewed fruit or jam or dress it up by filling a well-oiled 0.5 litre (1 pint) ring mould lined with clingfilm. When set, unmould onto a serving plate and fill the centre with fresh fruit, such as raspberries or blackberries or cooked apples or apricots.

PEARS

Pears have always flourished in England. We grow Jargonelle, a very old variety, on a north wall and have found it is best eaten while still crisp, like an apple. Durondeau is another old variety which cooks to a delicate shell-pink with honey. Cooking pears, like the nuggetty local Black Worcester, are notoriously hard and only respond to hours of slow stewing, but have the advantage of keeping well. The ripeness of dessert pears, on the other hand, has to be judged very carefully as they are often at their peak for only one day, quickly becoming sleepy.

The old zinc nameplates, their lettering faint and faded, are still attached in places to the high brick walls inside and out of our kitchen garden, relics of an absorbing gardening past. John Skyppe's diary, recording the walled garden he built in Ledbury in the 1690s, listed dozens of varieties of apples, pears, cherries and plums, as well as peaches and apricots, most of them unknown today. But it is still a common sight, especially in Herefordshire, to see an ancient pear tree trained on a warm cottage or farmhouse wall, bridal white in the Spring and laden with choice fruits in the Autumn.

GRILLED HONEYED PEARS

SERVES: 6
PREPARATION TIME: 10 minutes
GRILLING TIME: 15 minutes

6 ripe dessert pears, such as William or Baron de Mello
juice of 1 lemon
55g (2 oz) unsalted butter, melted
3 tablespoonsful honey
ginger ice cream to serve

1 Peel the pears, halve and scoop out the core with a teaspoon. Brush all over with lemon juice and lay, cut-side down, on a grill rack – line the tray with aluminium foil.
Brush thoroughly with some of the melted butter.
2 Grill under a medium heat for 10 minutes or so, until the pears begin to brown. Turn the pears over, brush with the remaining butter and drop some honey into each hollow. Grill the pears again until the honey bubbles and the pears are lightly browned. Serve hot with ginger ice cream.

These pears are also delicious served cold, but they do not keep well for more than an hour or two.

PEARS POACHED IN PERRY

PREPARATION TIME: 10 minutes
BAKING TIME: 3–4 hours

6 ripe pears, such as Durondeau or Conference
fresh vine leaves
juice of ½ lemon
2 tablespoonsful golden granulated sugar
½ cinnamon stick
I pint perry
fresh whipped cream to serve

1 Peel, halve and core the pears. If they are small, leave them whole with the stalk intact.
2 Lay them on a bed of fresh vine leaves, keeping a few of the smallest leaves for decoration, in a heavy casserole. Sprinkle with lemon juice and sugar, put in the cinnamon stick, cover with perry and fit the lid on tight.
3 Heat the oven to 275–300°F/140–150°C/Gas mark 1–2 and stew for 3–4 hours, or until the pears have softened enough to eat. From time to time, check there is enough liquid in the casserole and top up if necessary. Transfer the pears to a serving dish.
Discard the cinnamon stick and vine leaves.
4 Strain the cooking juices into a clean pan and boil down the liquid to make a syrup.
5 Serve the pears with the syrup and whipped cream decorated with small vine leaves, or the pears as a filling for meringues or cream cake.

CHESTNUT AND PEAR FLAN

We are fortunate to have a row of extremely venerable, large Spanish chestnuts within sight of the kitchen. Elizabeth Barrett Browning wrote about them when she lived here. They were well grown even then.

Underneath the chestnuts dripping
Through the grasses wet and fair,
Straight I sought my garden-ground
With the laurel on the mound
And the pear-tree oversweeping, a side shadow of green air.

This gave me the idea for a chestnut and pear flan. The chestnuts, though plentiful, are often rather small. I find that dried chestnuts do very well, but they are not as good as the fresh ones after a warm summer. Soak the dried chestnuts overnight if possible to reduce the cooking time.

SERVES: 6
SOAKING TIME: (optional) overnight
PREPARATION TIME: making the pastry,
plus 20 minutes
RESTING TIME: 30 minutes
BAKING TIME: 15 minutes
COOKING TIME: 1¼–2½ hours
(depending on whether the chestnuts were soaked)

90g (3 oz) wholemeal shortcrust pastry (page 176)

FILLING

115g (4 oz) dried chestnuts
3–4 large dessert pears
425 ml (¾ pint) dry perry
1 vanilla pod
3 tablespoonsful honey
redcurrant or medlar jelly to glaze
fresh thick Jersey cream to serve

1 Soak the chestnuts overnight if possible, as this will cut down appreciably on the cooking time.

2 Allow the pastry to rest for 30 minutes in a cool place. Roll out and bake blind, following the directions on page 176.

3 Peel, halve and core the pears. Put them into a saucepan with the perry and poach until lightly cooked. Timing will depend on the ripeness of the pears, but allow about 15 minutes. When they are done, lift them out with a slotted spoon and allow to cool.

4 Drain the chestnuts and simmer in the pear poaching liquid with the vanilla pod. This could take up to 2 hours if they are very hard to start with. Top up with water if necessary.

5 When the chestnuts are cooked, remove the vanilla pod and process with the honey and enough of the cooking liquid to produce a smooth purée.

6 Spread the chestnut purée over the pastry base and arrange the poached pears on top, cut-side down, glaze with the red fruit jelly, melted in a bowl over hot water, and serve with thick, golden Jersey cream.

COFFEE BLANCMANGE WITH
CHOCOLATE SAUCE

Blancmange has suffered the caprices of fortune. Originating in medieval times and rising to a crescendo of popularity in the Victorian and Edwardian eras, it has now been relegated to a more humble position. Blancmange buffs, however, relish the smooth, unctuous texture, the slight pull on the tongue, the distinct, rather than bland flavour.

I have evolved a method of combining cornflour and gelatine, both used historically in the preparation of blancmange, which alleviates any stodginess. We are also lucky to have full-cream goat's milk available, which makes another great difference.

SERVES: 6
PREPARATION TIME: 30 minutes
COOKING TIME: 15 minutes
SETTING TIME: 1–2 hours

570ml (1 pint) fresh milk (goat's milk for preference)
30g (1 oz) freshly-ground coffee
2 leaves gelatine
30g (1 oz) cornflour
55g (2 oz) light muscovado sugar

CHOCOLATE SAUCE

100g (3½ oz) bitter chocolate
90ml (3 fl oz) hot water or fresh milk
fresh whipped cream to serve
grated chocolate or praline (page 46) to decorate

1 Warm the milk and infuse the coffee for 15 minutes, then strain through.
2 Soak the gelatine in a little cold water. Mix the cornflour to a paste with a little of the flavoured milk and the sugar. Heat 285ml (½ pint) of the remaining milk in a saucepan, combine with the cornflour paste and tip back into the saucepan over a moderate heat. Stir vigorously until the mixture thickens. Remove from the heat and allow to cool.
3 Warm the rest of the milk to blood heat and dissolve the softened gelatine leaves in it. When the cornflour mixture is cool, stir into the gelatine milk, whisking well together. Pour into individual glasses and leave to set in the refrigerator for 1–2 hours.

4 To make the chocolate sauce, break up the chocolate in a small basin over a saucepan of boiling water until it has just melted. Off the heat add the hot water or milk, stirring it well until smooth.

5 Serve the blancmange with the chocolate sauce and a spoonful of whipped cream, and grated chocolate or praline.

DAW CHUTNEY

My grandfather had a vinegar brewery and, later, fruit farms and was always experimenting with new ways to use his products. DAW Chutney, so-called because it was 'Delicious, Appetising and Wholesome' and which sported a jaunty jackdaw in profile on the labels of its green glass bottles, combined these interests.

MAKES: approximately 2.7kg (6 lb)
PREPARATION TIME: 30 times
COOKING TIME: 30–40 minutes

1.8kg (4 lb) tart apples	340g (¾ lb) dark muscovado sugar
170g (6 oz) onions	1 tablespoonful pickling spice
8 cloves garlic	½ teaspoonful cayenne pepper
425ml (¾ pint) cider vinegar	1 teaspoonful coriander seeds
340g (¾ lb) dates, stoned and chopped	30g (1 oz) piece fresh root ginger, quartered
170g (6 oz) sultanas or raisins	sea salt (optional)

1 Peel, core and slice the apples. Peel and chop the onions and garlic. Tip both into a heavy-based saucepan containing half the vinegar and simmer until tender, 10–15 minutes.
2 Add the dates, sultanas or raisins, sugar, pickling spice, cayenne pepper, coriander seeds and ginger, fresh if possible, since it has more zing and fragrance, and the remainder of the vinegar. Simmer all the ingredients together until the mixture is good and thick, about 20 minutes. Remove from the heat.
3 Extract the root ginger, season with salt if you wish and pot into warm sterilized jars. If the jars have metal lids, protect them with vinegar-proof paper and make certain the jars are sealed tightly, as vinegar evaporates easily and the chutney might become unappetizingly dry.

AUTUMN MENUS

SIMPLE SUPPER

Pike and Chive Mayonnaise (page 109)

Beef in Mustard and Savoury Sauce (page 117)
Marrow with Ginger Butter (page 118)
Spinach
Riced Potatoes (page 25)

Pears Poached in Perry (133)

VEGETARIAN SUPPER OR LIGHT LUNCH

Lovage Soup (page 101)

Navarin of Autumn Vegetables (page 112)
Spiced Rice (page 74)

Coffee Blancmange (page 136)

DINNER PARTY

Pumpkin and Saffron Soup (page 103)

Dill Pork (page 114)
Mixed Autumn Vegetables
Soufflé Potatoes (page 28)

Apple and Fennel Salad (page 121)

Grilled Honeyed Pears (page 132) with
Barley Kernel Pudding (page 130)
Mulberry and Melon (page 122)

WINTER

DECEMBER, JANUARY, FEBRUARY

*E*ach year I forget how long winter is — five cold months of cold or wet, the snow and ice and short, dark days. How enjoyable are those few bright, sparkling moments when we can prune our roses and apple trees with pleasure! The crackling frosts and driving rain break up the earth and make it friable, ready for new planting.

Sometimes I wish I could hibernate like a dormouse, but then I would lose the opportunity to exploit the wealth of the year which has gone before. I like to think of these vegetables and the logs burning brightly on the fire as so much stored sunlight from last year.

And, as always, there is that ancient feast, pagan then Christian, to start a new year and provide the watershed between darkness and light.

JERUSALEM ARTICHOKE AND FENNEL SOUP

A white soup for winter – Jerusalem artichokes are easy to grow and fennel is imported throughout this season. The two vegetables are an interesting combination; a change from the more usual winter roots.

SERVES: 6
PREPARATION TIME: 20 minutes
COOKING TIME: 25 minutes

30g (1 oz) unsalted butter
1 medium-sized onion, chopped
225g (½ lb) fresh Jerusalem artichokes
1 Florence fennel bulb
900ml (1½ pints) hot ham or chicken stock
1 teaspoonful fennel seeds
140ml (¼ pint) fresh single cream
sea salt
freshly ground black pepper
paprika and fennel fronds to garnish
garlic croûtons to serve

1 Melt the butter in a large saucepan. Add the onion and cook over a low heat until it is transparent.

2 Peel and slice the artichokes and slice the fennel, reserving any bright green fronds for the garnish. Add the artichokes, fennel and stock to the saucepan and simmer until the vegetables are soft.

3 Meanwhile, grind the fennel seeds with a pestle and mortar and add to the saucepan.

4 Liquidize till smooth.

5 Pour back into the cleaned saucepan – through a sieve if you prefer a silky, smooth soup – and add the cream and salt and pepper to taste.

6 Serve very hot, speckled with paprika, snippets of fennel frond and garlic croutons.

SHALLOT AND PARSLEY SOUP

Shallots are a wonderful vegetable, storing all through the winter until they are replanted in March and April. I use them constantly as a base for sauces and for this delicious soup, which also utilizes the parsley that survives in the greenhouse.

SERVES: 6
PREPARATION TIME: 15 minutes
COOKING TIME: 20 minutes

170g (6 oz) shallots
1 medium-sized potato
55g (2 oz) unsalted butter
1.1 litre (2 pints) hot chicken or ham stock or game stock
handful of fresh English parsley
freshly ground black pepper

1 Peel and slice the shallots and potato.
2 Melt the butter in a large saucepan over a moderate heat, add the shallots and potato and cook for a few moments. Pour in the stock, bring to a simmer and cook until the potato is tender. Remove from the heat and allow to cool slightly.
3 Liquidize the vegetables and stock with half the parsley, so the soup turns a pretty green.
4 Chop the remaining parsley fairly finely and stir into the soup. Reheat if necessary. Season with plenty of pepper and serve with wholemeal bread and butter.

HEARTY VEGETABLE SOUP

I like this very simple soup, which is so easy to make with ingredients that are always to hand.

SERVES: 6
PREPARATION TIME: 15 minutes
COOKING TIME: 20–30 minutes

2 medium-sized onions
3 medium-sized carrots
2 medium-sized potatoes
85g (3 oz) unsalted butter
6 medium-sized tomatoes
I tablespoonful tomato purée
1.1 litre (2 pints) hot chicken, duck or vegetable stock
I bay leaf
sea salt or celery salt
freshly ground black pepper
a little fresh milk (optional)

1 Peel and slice the onions, carrots and potatoes.
2 Melt the butter in a large saucepan over a low heat and cook the prepared vegetables gently for 10 minutes.
3 Meanwhile, chop the tomatoes, then add to the saucepan with the tomato purée. Pour on the stock, add the bay leaf and simmer until all the vegetables are soft, about 10–20 minutes.
4 Remove the bay leaf and liquidize the mixture. Sieve the soup back into the rinsed out saucepan, season with salt or celery salt and pepper and reheat gently, stirring and adding a little milk if the soup is too thick.
5 When the soup is served, really hot, embellish it with a swirl of yogurt and a sprinkling of paprika. Or make the most of any snippets of winter greenery you can find such as celery leaves, fine strips of raw leek or spinach or green peppers. The tiniest patch of green enhances the appearance quite dramatically.

SPINACH AND PRAWN PANCAKES

Spinach is available all the year round. This recipe is a very good way to make the most of the expensive and comparatively rare delicacy of fresh prawns.

SERVES: 6
PREPARATION TIME: 10 minutes
COOKING TIME: 20–25 minutes
BAKING TIME: 8 minutes or
GRILLING TIME: 5–8 minutes

Pancake batter (see Asparagus Pancakes, page 19)

FILLING

455g (1 lb) fresh spinach

115g (4 oz) curd cheese

freshly grated nutmeg

sea salt

freshly ground black pepper

340g (¾ lb) fresh prawns, cooked and peeled

120ml (4 fl oz) thick natural yogurt

handful of pine kernels

freshly grated Parmesan cheese

1 First make the batter, using the ingredients and method for Asparagus Pancakes (page 19).
2 Wash the spinach, removing the hard stems. Put the slightly damp leaves into a heavy saucepan and cook until they have reduced and softened, about 5 minutes. Leave to cool.
3 When the spinach is cool enough to handle, squeeze out any excess moisture and cut across several times in different directions with a sharp knife. Fork in the curd cheese, nutmeg and salt and pepper to taste. Mix the prawns, reserving the 12 most shapely for decoration.
4 Preheat the oven to 450°F/230°C/Gas mark 8 or heat the grill to moderate.
5 Fill the centre of each pancake with a thick seam of spinach mixture, fold the pancakes over the filling and arrange on a greased baking tray. Spread a band of yogurt over the pancakes, arrange 2 prawns back to back on each and emboss with pine nuts. Scatter with Parmesan cheese and bake for about 8 minutes or grill for about 5–8 minutes, until the pine kernels are browned and the yogurt has turned lacy and bubbling.

SALSIFY AND SCORZONERA

We have grown salsify and scorzonera side by side in our garden and I have found salsify has the more distinctive flavour, while black-skinned scorzonera is easier to peel. The skins of both slip off more neatly after they are cooked, but the water is too discoloured to use for stock. The alternative is to scrape off the skin painstakingly first, putting the cleaned pieces into acidulated water to keep them white.

Cooked and served with a dressing of butter and lemon and plenty of freshly ground black pepper, it partners beef particularly well. Or it can be sliced and fried in olive oil or bacon fat, then lightly sprinkled with lemon juice and parsley to accompany roast poultry or game.

VEGETABLE OYSTER AND WALNUTS

A slightly more elaborate dish, which can stand on its own, is made by swathing the salsify in a cheese and walnut sauce.

SERVES: 6
PREPARATION TIME: 15 minutes
COOKING TIME: 35 minutes
BAKING TIME: 15 minutes

1.1kg (2½ lb) fresh salsify
1 tablespoonful lemon sauce

CHEESE AND WALNUT SAUCE

2 tablespoonsful chicken, duck or goose fat
2 cloves garlic crushed with a little sea salt
45g (1½ oz) wholemeal flour
140ml (¼ pint) dry white wine
140ml (¼ pint) salsify stock (see below)
55g (2 oz) farmhouse Cheddar cheese
1 tablespoonful freshly grated Parmesan cheese
55g (2 oz) walnuts
1 tablespoonful chopped fresh winter savory
sea salt
freshly ground black pepper
2 tablespoonsful wholemeal breadcrumbs
30g (1 oz) unsalted butter

1 Break off the small side roots of the salsify and discard. Wash the main roots. Scrape off the brown skin, putting the cleaned pieces into water acidulated with the lemon juice to keep the salsify white. Or cook first then peel.

2 Drain the salsify, put into a saucepan and cover with cold water. Bring to the boil over a moderate heat, then simmer until the roots are tender, about 30 minutes. Reserve 140ml (¼ pint) of the cooking liquid for the sauce, then drain and cut the roots on the bias into 1.25cm (½-inch) pieces. Set aside.

3 Preheat the oven to 400°F/200°C/Gas mark 6. Make the sauce. Melt the poultry fat into a small saucepan over a low heat, add the garlic crushed with the salt and stir in the flour. Cook for 1 minute. Mix in the wine and stock and cook until the sauce thickens.

4 Stir most of the cheeses, the walnuts, salsify and winter savory into the sauce and season to taste. Tip into a wide earthenware dish. Mix the breadcrumbs with the remaining cheese, sprinkle over the top and dot with butter. Cook until the top is brown and bubbling.

CARDOONS

An 'avenue' of silvery glaucous green cardoons, nearly six feet high, is a stately backcloth for the early Winter garden. The stems should be blanched by binding them round with thick brown paper. They are related to the globe artichoke and the stems have that same mealy texture reminiscent of artichoke hearts. The flavour is strange and elusive, delicate to our modern palates. Like seakale, another old fashioned plant, it pairs beautifully with ham or seafood.

Treat cardoons like celery to prepare. Trim the plant to about 38cm (15 inches).

Cut off the thick stump and discard the outer stalks. Use only these blanched inner stalks with their lovely satiny sheen making sure you cut off any leaves and prickles.

It is usual to cook the chopped cardoon in a little water for about 15 minutes to lose any bitterness, discarding the water afterwards. However, I have found with our own cardoons this is not always necessary and indeed find a slight bitterness rather attractive. The tangy cooking liquor makes a good stock.

CARDOON BOATS

SERVES: 6
PREPARATION TIME: 20 minutes
COOKING TIME: 25 minutes
BAKING TIME: 15 minutes

4–6 inner cardoon stalks
455g (1 lb) ripe tomatoes
2 tablespoonsful water
1 tablespoonful tomato purée
1 tin anchovies
sea salt if needed
1 teaspoonful green peppercorns
3 tablespoonsful wholemeal breadcrumbs

1 Cut the cardoons into 7.5cm (3-inch) 'boats'.

2 Drop the cardoons into a saucepan of boiling water and cook for about 15 minutes until just firm to bite. Drain, reserving the stock for sauces or soup, and set the cardoons aside.

3 Chop the tomatoes, and soften them in a pan with the water, about 10 minutes. Push them through a sieve. Add the tomato purée and the oil from the anchovies. Season with salt if it is needed.

4 Preheat the oven to 400°F/200°C/Gas mark 6. Arrange the cardoons in a single layer in a shallow ovenproof dish. Fill the 'boats' with the tomato sauce and lay an anchovy over each one. Grind the peppercorns with a pestle and mortar, mix with the breadcrumbs and sprinkle over the tops of the cardoons. Bake for 15 minutes until nicely heated through or finish off under a hot grill for 2 minutes.

You could also serve the cooked cardoon 'boats' cold, filled with crab meat, dressed with a herb mayonnaise. Tarragon is particularly nice.

CARDOON IN HAM AND MUSTARD SAUCE

Another way of bringing out the complementary flavours of cardoon and ham is to combine them in a mustard sauce. Very nice as a supper dish.

SERVES: 6

PREPARATION TIME: 10 minutes

COOKING TIME: 20 minutes

455g (1 lb) inner cardoon stalks
225g (½ lb) ham (traditionally reared and cured if possible)
30g (1 oz) unsalted butter
30g (1 oz) wholemeal flour
140ml (¼ pint) cardoon stock (see below)
140ml (½ pint) strong bitter ale
1 tablespoonful made English mustard
3 tablespoonsful fresh double cream
sea salt
freshly ground black pepper

1 Chop the cardoon into 1.25cm (½-inch) dice. Toss into boiling water and cook for 10 minutes. Drain, reserving the stock for the sauce. Cut the ham into matching dice.

2 Make the sauce. Melt the butter in a saucepan over a low heat, stir in the flour and cook for 1 minute. Add the stock and ale and increase the heat. Keep stirring until the sauce is bubbling and thick, then add the mustard, cream and seasoning. Stir in the cardoon and ham and heat through.

3 Serve hot on wholemeal toast or with potatoes, steamed in their skins, well-buttered and scattered with fresh parsley.

CARDOON WITH CHESTNUTS

Chestnuts, brought to England by the Romans, go remarkably well with many winter vegetables, such as Brussels sprouts, cabbage and celery. They also have an outstanding affinity with game and poultry. This simple cardoon dish is a particularly apt accompaniment to roast pheasant or guinea fowl.

SERVES: 6
PREPARATION TIME: minimal
COOKING TIME: 15 minutes

455g (1 lb) inner cardoon stalks
2 tablespoonsful virgin olive oil
225g (½ lb) chestnuts, cooked
juice of 1/2 lemon

1 Cut the cardoon stalks into 1.25cm (½-inch) dice.
2 Cook the cardoon dice in boiling water for 10 minutes. Drain, reserving the stock for sauces or soup.
3 Heat the oil in a large frying pan over a moderate heat. Turn the cardoons and chestnuts over in the oil until lightly fried. Squeeze over the lemon juice and serve.

BEEFY CARDOON PIE

This is a main meal dish with light ingredients under a rich pastry crust. The stock from the bones is used to cook the cardoons and the marrow from the long bones with its subtle, delicate flavour strengthens the sauce and goes astonishingly well with this vegetable.

SERVES: 6
COOKING TIME: 3 hours
PREPARATION TIME: Making the pastry,
plus 15 minutes
BAKING TIME: 25 minutes

MARROW BONE STOCK

4 beef marrow bones, the straight pieces cut into
7.5cm (3-inch) lengths
1 onion, peeled and halved
1 teaspoonful black peppercorns
1 bay leaf
1 recipe quantity Wholemeal Puff Pastry (page 177) ·

FILLING

340g (¾ lb) fresh inner cardoon stalks
285ml (½ pint) reduced marrow bone stock (see opposite)
340g (¾ lb) fresh mushrooms
30g (1 oz) unsalted butter
2 cloves garlic
pinch of sea salt

SAUCE

55g (2 oz) unsalted butter
55g (2 oz) wholemeal flour
570ml (1 pint) reduced marrow bone stock (see opposite)
285ml (½ pint) Newcastle brown ale
1 tablespoon tamari
freshly ground black pepper

1 Make the marrow bone stock first. Reserve 6 of the 7.5cm (3-inch) straight lengths of bone. Put the remainder in a large stock-pot and cover with cold water. Bring slowly to the boil, skim the scum off the surface and simmer for 1 hour.

2 Meanwhile, prepare the pastry, if you have not already done so and chill in the refrigerator until needed.

3 After the stock has simmered for 1 hour, remove from the heat and pour off 1.1 litres (2 pints) into a saucepan. Reduce by half, by boiling it quickly with the onion, bay leaf and peppercorns. When done, strain the stock. Unless I am going to use a stock immediately, I omit the onion as it affects the keeping quality of the stock. You will need half this stock for the pie filling, and half for the sauce.

4 Put the reserved marrow bones in one or two boilable plastic pudding basins, clip on the lid and cook in boiling water for 1½ hours, topping up the boiling water as necessary. When done, extract the marrow for use in the sauce and discard the bones.

5 Chop the cardoon sticks into 2.5cm (1-inch) lengths. Cook in half the reduced stock until just soft, about 10–15 minutes, then drain, reserving any liquor for the sauce. Cut the mushrooms into pieces about the same size as the cardoons and cook gently in the butter for a minute or two with the garlic, which has been crushed with the salt in a pestle and mortar.

6 Make the sauce. Melt the butter in a saucepan, add the flour and cook for 1 minute. Stir in the rest of the reserved reduced stock, any liquor remaining from cooking the cardoons, the ale and beef pieces, and bubble for about 2 minutes, remove from the heat and add the tamari and pepper to taste.

7 Combine the cardoon, mushrooms and sauce, pile into a 1 litre (1½–2 pint) pie dish and allow to cool.

8 Preheat the oven to 400°F/200°C/Gas mark 6. Roll out the pastry and fit over the pie as a lid, using any pastry scraps to make decorative leaves and fruit. Cut a steam hole in the pastry and bake for 25 minutes. Serve hot.

Cardoon Curd Crust

Really tangy tomatoes, like Ailsa Craig, give a spectacular flavour to this vegetarian dish.

SERVES: 6
PREPARATION TIME: 10 minutes
COOKING TIME: 40 minutes
BAKING TIME: 30 minutes

FILLING	CURD CRUST
340g (12 oz) inner cardoon stalks	285g (10 oz) curd
I tablespoonful cider vinegar or lemon juice	3 free-range eggs
30g (I oz) unsalted butter	sea salt
55g (2 oz) onion chopped	freshly ground black pepper
2 cloves garlic, crushed	2 tablespoonsful freshly grated Parmesan cheese or
680g (1½ lb) ripe tomatoes	finely grated farmhouse Cheddar cheese
4 tablespoonsful Herefordshire dry cider	
I tablespoonful Worcestershire sauce	
2 tablespoonsful chopped fresh English parsley	

1 Cut the cardoon stalks into 5cm (2-inch) pieces. Bring a saucepan of water to the boil, add the vinegar or lemon juice and cook the cardoon pieces until just tender, about 20 minutes. Remove from the heat, peel off any stringy bits and pack into a 1 litre (1½–2 pint) gratin dish.

2 Melt the butter in a saucepan over gentle heat. Soften the onion and garlic, about 5 minutes, then add the tomatoes. Cook for a further 5 minutes. Sieve, return to the pan, add the cider and Worcester sauce and reduce until thick. Stir in the parsley and spread the sauce over the cardoons.

3 Preheat the oven to 450°F/230°C/Gas mark 8.

4 Process the curd, eggs, half the Parmesan or Cheddar cheese and seasoning, then smooth the thick, creamy paste evenly over the vegetables and sauce. Sprinkle with the remaining cheese.

5 Bake for 10 minutes, reduce the heat to 375°F/190°C/Gas mark 5 and bake for a further 20 minutes, until the curd has puffed up and turned golden.

OYSTERS IN A CHABLIS SAUCE

Ideal as a starter or special supper dish. Oysters are in season from September to April and are a treat these days. Once they were plentiful and cheap; their present scarcity is the unfortunate result of disease and pollution.

In this recipe, the mellow scrambled egg helps them to go further as well as providing a foil for their delicate salty tang and the crispness of the toast.

SERVES: 6
PREPARATION TIME: 30 minutes
COOKING TIME: 15 minutes

approximately 24 oysters in their shell (depending on size)
I bottle Chablis
6 rounds wholemeal bread, lightly toasted
3 tablespoonful cold-pressed olive oil
55g (2 oz) unsalted butter
6 free-range eggs, beaten
I tablespoonful chopped fresh English parsley
pinch of sea salt
cayenne pepper (optional)
fresh English parsley sprigs to garnish

1 Open the oysters yourself with a proper oyster knife, putting the tip of the knife between the shells on the flat edge and giving it a twist – there is a knack to it! – or ask your fishmonger to do it for you. Either way, try to conserve the precious juices.

2 Strain the juices into a small saucepan, add 6 tablespoonful Chablis and reduce until only 6 tablespoonful liquor remains.

3 Trim the toasts and fry in the olive oil until crisp on both sides. Remove from the pan and keep warm. Melt the butter in a medium saucepan and scramble the eggs slowly, stirring all the time. Be very careful to leave them creamy – do not overcook. Mix in the parsley and sea salt.

4 Drop the oysters into the juice for a few seconds to warm them. Make a nest by using the toast as a base and covering with a portion of scrambled egg. Place 4 oysters and approximately 1 tablespoonful sauce in each 'nest' and sprinkle a little cayenne judiciously over the top if using. Decorate with parsley sprigs and enjoy with the rest of the bottle of Chablis.

SCALLOPS IN SAFFRON AND YOGURT SAUCE

The image of the scallop shell has entranced philosophers, painters and poets. It was the symbolic motif of pilgrims, the inspiration for architects and craftsmen. In the humbler context of the kitchen, the scallop is a delight to the eye and the palate.

The saffron, much used in old English recipes, imparts a gentle fragrance, the yogurt contributes a creamy sharpness to this dish which glows with colour.

SERVES: 6
PREPARATION TIME: 15 minutes
COOKING TIME: 30 minutes
GRILLING TIME: 5 minutes

12–18 scallops in their shell (keep 6 shells for serving)
180ml (6 fl oz) dry cider

SAFFRON AND YOGURT SAUCE

1 pinch saffron strands soaked in 1 tablespoonful water
140ml (¼ pint) natural yogurt
55g (2 oz) unsalted butter
2 tablespoonful wholemeal flour
3 egg yolks
2 tablespoonful sherry (optional)

TOMATO SAUCE

6 ripe tomatoes
1 clove garlic, crushed with a little sea salt
freshly ground black pepper
chopped fresh English parsley to garnish
2 tablespoonful finely grated farmhouse Cheddar cheese or
freshly grated Parmesan cheese

1 Separate the white part of the scallops from the corals. Reserve the corals and poach the scallops in a saucepan with the cider for 5 minutes. Remove from the heat, lift out the scallops with a slotted spoon. Reserve the cooking liquor.

2 Mix the dyed saffron liquid into the yogurt. Melt half the butter in a saucepan, stir in the flour – the yogurt will separate without it – cook for 1 minute and add the scallop cooking liquor. Simmer for 5 minutes, then sieve and add the yogurt, sherry, if using it, and egg yolks. Stir well and season to taste.

3 Skin, deseed and chop the tomatoes. Put into a saucepan over gentle heat and cook until well heated through with the garlic and remaining butter. Add the corals and cook for a further 3 minutes.

4 Heat the grill to medium. Reheat the scallops gently in the yogurt sauce and place in the scallop shells. Arrange the corals in tomato sauce in the centre of each shell or as a brilliant rim. Scatter over the cheese and brown under the grill until the cheese melts and everything is hot, about 5–8 minutes. Garnish with a tuft of parsley and serve with wholemeal bread and butter.

PIKE DUMPLINGS WITH DILL AND TOMATO SAUCE

Dill and tomato are superb together. Dill seeds vary greatly in strength depending on their freshness. Tomatoes frozen at the peak of their flavour are ideal for this sauce.

The pike dumplings can be prepared beforehand, so that all there remains to do is to heat them up in the sauce under the grill.

SERVES: 8 as a starter
PREPARATION TIME: approximately 30 minutes
COOKING TIME: 30–40 minutes
GRILLING TIME: 10 minutes

DUMPLINGS

1.5–2kg (3–4 lb) pike
4 egg whites
240ml (8 fl oz) fresh double cream
grated nutmeg
pinch of sea salt

SAUCE

680g (1½ lb) ripe tomatoes
1 tablespoonful dill seeds, or to taste
30g (1 oz) unsalted butter
30g (1 oz) wholemeal flour
2 tablespoonsful freshly grated Parmesan cheese
120ml (4 fl oz) fresh single cream
sea salt
freshly ground black pepper
wholemeal breadcrumbs
fresh dill to garnish

1 Skin and fillet the fish, teasing out the bones, to obtain 455g (1 lb) flesh. Chop into 2.5cm (1-inch) pieces and process thoroughly with the egg white. Work in the cream, nutmeg and salt to taste but just until well-combined or it might become buttery. Chill the mixture in the refrigerator until you are ready to poach the dumplings.

2 Make the sauce. In a medium-sized saucepan, cook the tomatoes with 2 tablespoonsful water over a low heat until soft, then sieve into a bowl.

3 Whizz the dill seeds in a liquidizer, then tip into the tomato purée. Mix well.

4 Melt the butter in a clean, medium-sized saucepan over a low heat, stir in the flour and cook for 1 minute. Add the tomato mixture and continue cooking until thick. Cook for a further 2–3 minutes, stirring or whisking constantly. Remove from the heat and add half the Parmesan cheese, cream and seasoning. Mix well.

5 To make the dumplings, heat a large saucepan of salted water to simmering point. Lower shaped dessertspoonsfuls of fish mixture into the water, a few at a time and poach for about 7 minutes. Lift the dumplings out with a slotted spoon, dry on absorbent kitchen paper and arrange in shallow fireproof dishes.

6 Heat the grill to medium. Pour some sauce over the dumplings, sprinkle with bread-crumbs and the remaining Parmesan cheese and grill for about 10 minutes, to colour and heat through. Decorate with fresh dill if available.

SALMI OF WILD DUCK

This recipe stretches back in an unbroken line to medieval times. It can be adapted for any game and Jane Grigson, in *English Food*, cites a 1430 version for fish.

SERVES: 6
ROASTING TIME: 30–40 minutes
COOKING TIME: approximately 1½ hours
PREPARATION TIME: 5 minutes

3 wild mallard ducks
6 rashers streaky bacon

SAUCE

570ml (1 pint) dry red wine
4 shallots, roughly chopped
1 bay leaf
few sprigs of fresh thyme
few sprigs of fresh English parsley
10 black peppercorns
4 slices orange peel, well scrubbed
1½ tablespoonsful cornflour
1 tablespoonful tamari

GARLIC MUSHROOMS

2 cloves garlic
sea salt
55g (2 oz) unsalted butter
115g (4 oz) fresh flat mushrooms
orange twists to garnish

1 Preheat the oven to 425°F/220°C/Gas mark 7. Cover the duck breasts with the bacon and roast for 30–40 minutes, depending on how you like your meat done. Remove from the oven and allow to cool off a little. Ease the breasts off the bone and set aside. Do not refrigerate.

2 Put the duck carcasses in a deep saucepan and cover with the wine, topping up with water. Bring to the boil and simmer for 1 hour. Strain off the stock into a clean saucepan. Add the shallots, bay leaf, thyme, parsley, peppercorns and orange peel. Reduce over a moderately-

high heat approximately 425ml (¾ pint). Thicken with the cornflour, mixed with a little wine or water to a paste, then add the tamari.

3 Crush the garlic with a little sea salt and fork into the butter. Melt the garlic butter in a frying pan and fry the mushrooms gently. Keep warm.

4 Skin the duck breasts, slicing them obliquely if you wish and warm in the sauce for 5–8 minutes. Avoid boiling as the breasts will stiffen and harden.

5 To serve, pour a little sauce around the duck breasts and decorate with the garlic, mushrooms and orange twists. Hand the remaining sauce round separately.

QUINCES

There is something old-fashioned, almost archaic, about the appearance of quinces, perhaps because they have never been developed like pears. They were a widely-grown and popular fruit as many old recipes testify, but somehow fell from fashion.

If you haven't had time to plant a quince tree, haven't inherited one and find your greengrocer looks at you with astonishment when you ask for quinces, apples or part apples can be substituted. Even one quince will impart its distinctive flavour to a dish. Prepared slices freeze quite well and need no preparatory cooking.

PHOTOGRAPHS:

Oysters in a Chablis Sauce
Cardoon Curd Crust; Cucumber and Apple Mint Salad
Roast Pork and Quince
Apple Pie; Apple, Quince and Honey Suet Crust

ROAST PORK AND QUINCE

SERVES: 6
PREPARATION TIME: 20 minutes
COOKING TIME: 15 minutes
BAKING TIME: 1¾ hours

1.4kg (3 lb) boneless loin of pork (traditionally-reared if possible) with the skin intact
sea salt
2 quinces
½ pint perry
1 tablespoonful of whole cloves
clear honey
12 black peppercorns, crushed with a pestle and mortar
3 tablespoonsful wholemeal breadcrumbs
30g (1 oz) wholemeal flour
quince jelly to serve

1 Remove the skin from the pork by cutting through the fat, leaving half attached to the meat in an even layer. Score the fat by cutting deep slashes in it and rub all over with sea salt. Put into a shallow roasting tin, fat-side down and reserve the skin for crackling.

2 Peel, slice and core the quinces. Put into a saucepan with a little perry over a gentle heat and cook until the quinces are tender. Strain and reserve the cooking juices.

3 Preheat the oven to 400°F/200°C/Gas mark 6. Lay the quinces over the inside of the joint, scatter with a few cloves and close the sides together securing the joint with string or skewers. Smear honey all over the fat, mix together the crushed peppercorns and breadcrumbs and press evenly over the honeyed fat. Dot with more cloves. Pour 140ml (¼ pint) of the reserved quince cooking juices into the roasting tin, cover with aluminium foil and roast for 1¾ hours, or until the juices run clear when pierced with a sharp knife. 20 minutes before the cooking time is up, remove the foil and put the prepared skin on a baking sheet on the highest shelf of the oven above the pork.

4 When the pork is cooked, remove from the oven and keep warm. Allow to settle before carving. Watch the crackling carefully and remove it when it is crisp and brittle. Keep warm.

5 Just before serving, carve the pork into thin slices. Spoon most of the fat from the roasting tin and sprinkle in the flour. Mix well. Add any additional quince cooking juice and enough perry to make 285ml (½ pint) gravy.

6 Serve the quince-stuffed pork with pieces of crackling, soufflé potatoes and brussels sprouts. Hand round the gravy and quince jelly separately.

THATCHED COTTAGE PIE

A humble dish, as its name implies, of minced beef under a thatch of mashed potato. But its simple appeal continues for a family meal on cold wintry day. This is my version using oatmeal, which gives it a lovely, creamy body and richer flavour.

SERVES: 6
PREPARATION TIME: 10 minutes
COOKING TIME: 35 minutes
BAKING TIME: 2 hours

FILLING

55g (2 oz) beef dripping	I bay leaf
680g (1½ lb) good-quality minced beef	sea salt
I medium-size onion, finely chopped	freshly ground black pepper
425ml (¾ pint) hot beef stock	
6 tablespoonsful rolled organic porridge oats	900g (2 lb) potatoes
2 tablespoonsful tomato purée	55g (2 oz) butter
I tablespoonful tamari	sea salt
I tablespoonful Worcestershire sauce	freshly ground black pepper

1 Preheat the oven to 300°F/150°C/Gas mark 2.
2 Melt the dripping in a heavy casserole and fry the beef over a moderate heat until thoroughly browned. Add the onion and stir in the remaining filling ingredients. Bring to simmering point, then remove from the heat, cover with a tightly-fitting lid, or aluminium foil and then the lid, and bake in the oven for 1½ hours until thick and rich. Adjust the seasoning, tip into an ovenproof dish and allow to cool. Increase the oven temperature to 400°F/200°C/Gas mark 6.
3 Meanwhile, peel the potatoes and boil until tender. Drain well and mash with the butter and salt to taste. When the mince mixture has cooled, cover with the potatoes – easier if the potatoes are still warm – in an even layer. Fork furrow patterns over the surface and grind some black pepper over the top. Bake for 30–40 minutes, the top should be nicely browned.
4 Dish up with carrots and cottager's kale.

CIVET OF VENISON

Sometimes I am offered local venison — from a culling or a deer that has browsed too freely through a cabbage crop. I like it hung for at least a fortnight, so that the meat is very tender, but one has to be careful not to let the gaminess become too pronounced, or the taste too high.

A civet is a stew. This method of cooking keeps the meat succulent. Venison can be rather dry and is best marinated before roasting or grilling. Juniper berries still grow wild, in the more remote places like Cumberland. It was once commonly used in the cooking of game.

SERVES: 6

PREPARATION TIME: 15 minutes

COOKING TIME: 30 minutes

BAKING TIME: 1 1/2–2 hours

900g (2 lb) boned haunch of venison	1 tablespoonful juniper berries, crushed
3 tablespoonsful cold pressed olive oil	115g (4 oz) fresh mushrooms, sliced
30g (1 oz) unsalted butter	sea salt
1 medium-sized onion, thinly sliced	freshly ground black pepper
2 cloves garlic, chopped	
1 stick celery, sliced	**GARNISH**
1 medium-sized carrot, diced	12 shallots or small onions
2 tablespoonsful wholemeal flour	1 tablespoonful unrefined light muscovado sugar
1 bottle strong ale	2 tablespoonsful cider vinegar
venison stock	6 slices wholemeal toast
1 bouquet garni (bay leaf, parsley and thyme sprigs	45g (1½ oz) bacon fat
tied together)	sprigs of fresh English parsley

1 Cut the venison into 2.5cm (1-inch) cubes.

2 Preheat the oven to 300°F/150°C/Gas mark 2.

3 Heat some of the oil in a heavy-based frying pan, brown the meat all over in two batches, and transfer to a heavy casserole. Add the remaining oil to the frying pan with the butter and stir-fry onion, garlic, celery and carrot. Sprinkle the vegetables with the flour, mix in the ale and cook to make a sauce. Pour over the venison and top up with stock to just cover. Add the bouquet garni, juniper berries, mushrooms and seasoning, bring to simmering point and cook in the oven for about 2 hours, testing the meat for tenderness after about 1½ hours.

4 Peel the shallots or onions and put into a saucepan over a moderate heat with some venison stock. Cook for 10 minutes. Add the sugar and vinegar and reduce the liquid quickly, so that the sugar caramelizes and coats the shallots. Do not allow them to burn.

Remove from the heat and keep warm.

5 Trim the toast and cut into triangles. Melt the bacon fat in a frying pan and fry the triangles until crisp. Keep them warm.

6 If you think the gravy is too thin, strain off and boil it down fast to reduce.

7 Serve, garnished with glazed shallots, triangles of toast and sprigs of parsley.

ONIONS IN MADEIRA

When vegetable stocks run low in Winter and early Spring, there are always onions to fall back on. Cooked in this way, the staple onion is transformed and elevates any dish with which it is served, beef or beans.

SERVES: 6
PREPARATION TIME: 5 minutes
COOKING TIME: 15 minutes

4 large onions
55g (2 oz) unsalted butter
1 bay leaf
3 tablespoonsful Madeira wine
sea salt
freshly ground black pepper
fresh winter savory, very finely chopped or parsley chopped
120ml (4 fl oz) fresh double cream (optional)

1 Slice the onions into rings.

2 Melt the butter in a large saucepan over a low heat and sweat the onions with the bay leaf until they become transparent. Add the Madeira and continue cooking, stirring occasionally, until the onions are soft. Season and throw in the winter savory – chopped very finely as it can be coarse and scratchy at this time of year – or the parsley. Stir in the cream, if using, and heat through. Serve immediately.

PENNY POTATOES

Our answer to chips and crisps. Olive oil is a light and extremely delicious cooking medium for this recipe. Also delectable, though richer and more pronounced, is a little tasty dripping from goose or duck. Best of all is the fat from cooked rashers of farmhouse ham. This is one of the benefits accruing from using a proper free-range pig. There was a time when the pig was valued as much for its sweet fat as for the lean.

SERVES: 6
PREPARATION TIME: 10 minutes
COOKING TIME: 10 minutes
BAKING TIME: 15–25 minutes

900g (2 lb) potatoes
2 tablespoonsful cold pressed olive oil
55g (2 oz) unsalted butter
sea salt

1 Peel the potatoes and parboil for about 10 minutes. Drain and cool, then cut into discs.
2 Preheat the oven to 400°F/200°C/Gas mark 6. Heat the oil and butter together in a roasting tin that will hold the potato slices in 1 layer. Arrange the potatoes in the tin and bake until crisp and brown. Season with sea salt and serve.

STIR-FRIED CABBAGE

Often in winter, when vegetables are at a premium, there is limited choice of green things. This recipe can fill an awkward gap. If the cabbage seems very hard and tough when it has been sliced, such as the white drum head variety, it may need blanching momentarily before frying.

I have stir-fried vegetables in a frying pan for many years although a wok is also useful. The cooking time depends on the vegetables, but they should be served the minute they are tender enough to eat.

SERVES: 6
PREPARATION TIME: 15 minutes
COOKING TIME: minimal

3 sticks celery
1 small cabbage
few fresh mushrooms
2 tablespoonsful virgin olive oil
fresh root ginger
2 tablespoonsful finely chopped fresh English parsley
toasted flaked almonds
celery salt

1 Cut the celery crossways into slices and slice the cabbage and mushrooms finely.
2 Heat the oil in a heavy-based frying pan. Turn the celery over in the oil, then add the cabbage and mushrooms, moving them around the pan all the time so they do not burn.
3 Lastly, grate in some root ginger with discretion and add the parsley and celery salt. When the vegetables are tender enough to eat but still a nice firm texture – try eating a little to test – transfer to a warmed serving dish. Sprinkle with almonds and serve straight away.

RED CABBAGE AND APPLE

Spicy red cabbage can be rather pungent. I find that adding a good proportion of apple makes a much less cabbagey and more acceptable dish – it certainly alleviates the cooking smells. Cooked in this way red cabbage tastes best with game, such as the Wild Duck Salmi on (page 160) or Civet of Venison on Page 164.

SERVES: 6

PREPARATION TIME: 20 minutes

COOKING TIME: 1–3 hours

I small red cabbage
2 large cooking apples
3 tablespoonsful water
3–4 tablespoonsful cider vinegar
6 whole cloves
½ cinnamon stick
ground mixed spice (optional)
2–3 tablespoonsful redcurrant jelly or 2–3 tablespoonsful
dark muscovado sugar
sea salt
freshly ground black pepper
chopped fresh English parsley to garnish

1 Shred the cabbage very finely. Peel, core and slice the apples.

2 Put the cabbage, apples, water, vinegar, cloves and cinnamon stick in a heavy saucepan with a tightly fitting lid and cook, over the lowest heat possible, for 1–3 hours, depending on the age and toughness of the cabbage. Stir occasionally and add a little more water if the cabbage appears to be drying out, or remove the lid if it seems too watery. I find that leaving out the jelly or sugar at this stage lessens the chance of burning.

3 When the cabbage is cooked add the redcurrant jelly or sugar and adjust the sweet and sour ratio if necessary. Likewise, if the spices have lost their potency during cooking, top up with some ground mixed spice. Season with salt and pepper and serve with green parsley chopped among the pink strands of cabbage.

SUNSET BEANS

In this dish, red kidney beans are cooked in a sweet and sour sauce and served on a round of yellow pumpkin. I use Buttercup pumpkin for this if I can, because of its beautiful flavour, but any ripe, golden-fleshed pumpkin would look effective. This is a satisfying and dressy recipe that is suitable for vegans.

SERVES: 6

SOAKING TIME: overnight

COOKING TIME: approximately 1 hour, 20 minutes

PREPARATION TIME: 15 minutes

225g (½ lb) dried red kidney beans	SAUCE
I medium-sized onion	2 tablespoons cornflour
2 cloves garlic	I tablespoonful tamari
sea salt	½ pint stock (made up from cooking liquor
2 medium-sized sweet red peppers, deseeded	of beans and water)
and diced	2 tablespoonsful tomato purée
6 tablespoonsful cold pressed olive oil	I tablespoonful dark muscovado sugar
	4 tablespoonsful cider vinegar
	6 slices Buttercup pumpkin cut 1.25cm
	(½-inch) thick
	chopped fresh English parsley to garnish

1 Soak the beans overnight to water to cover.

2 Drain the beans, put into a saucepan, cover with fresh water and boil rapidly for 15 minutes over a high heat. Reduce the heat and cook for a further 45 minutes or until the beans are tender. Remove from the heat and drain, reserving the cooking liquor.

3 Slice the onion finely. Crush the garlic with a little sea salt and cook both in a small saucepan with 3 tablespoonsful of the oil until transparent, about 5 minutes. Meanwhile, mix the cornflour with the remaining sauce ingredients in a bowl.

4 Trim off the pumpkin rinds and deseed. Heat the remaining olive oil in a frying pan over a moderate heat and fry the pumpkin until crisp and golden-brown, about 10 minutes. Keep warm.

5 Combine the beans, onion, garlic and peppers in a saucepan. Pour over the sauce, bring to the boil over a moderate heat and cook for 2 minutes, stirring all the time. Season if necessary.

6 To serve, spoon helpings of beans over the pumpkin 'toast' and scatter with chopped English parsley.

Chestnut and Haricot Bean Casserole

This is a substantial main course dish for vegetarians or a warming supper dish. Haricot beans are easy to grow in the garden during sunny summers and are usually dried undercover in an airy place. If they are grown and dried at home, they will not take so long to cook as bought beans, which can be of indeterminate age.

SERVES: 6
SOAKING TIME: overnight
COOKING TIME: 2–2½ hours
BAKING TIME: 1 hour

170g (6 oz) dried chestnuts
170g (6 oz) dried haricot beans
570–900ml (1–1½ pints) dry cider
2 cloves garlic
1 medium-sized onion
30g (1 oz) unsalted butter
455g (1 lb) ripe tomatoes
2 tablespoonful water
2 teaspoonful tomato purée
1 tablespoonful unsulphured blackstrap molasses
1 tablespoonful tamari
1 bay leaf
sea salt
freshly ground black pepper
2 tablespoonful chopped fresh sweet marjoram

1 Soak the chestnuts overnight if possible. Drain, then put into a saucepan, cover with fresh water and cook over a moderate heat for 30 minutes, or until soft enough to bite through easily, but not crumbly.

2 Cover the haricot beans with cold water and bring to the boil over a moderate heat. Remove from the heat, cover the saucepan with a lid and leave for 2 hours. Drain the soaking water – this makes the beans more digestible – cover with cider and cook, tightly covered, over a low heat until the beans are almost tender, about 1½–2 hours.

3 Preheat the oven to 300°F/150°C/Gas mark 2. Chop the garlic and onion and put into a saucepan with the butter. Soften over a low heat, about 5 minutes. In another pan, cook the tomatoes with the water until soft, sieve and stir into the onion and garlic. Add the tomato purée, molasses, tamari and bay leaf. Season and put all the ingredients, including the chestnuts and beans, in a casserole and mix together. Bake for 1 hour, or until the chestnuts and beans are tender. Ten minutes before the end of baking time, stir in the marjoram.

CHICORY AND ORANGE SALAD

Always a lovely salad, especially after a rich stew or game dish. Keep the watercress in water in the refrigerator with damped leaves for a few hours before it is needed.

SERVES: 6
PREPARATION TIME: 10–15 minutes

6 small or 4 large Witloof chicons
6 sweet oranges
2 bunches watercress
I tablespoonful pine kernels

DRESSING

I tablespoonful sesame oil
2 teaspoonsful cold pressed olive oil
I teaspoonful cider vinegar or orange juice to taste

1 Slice the chicory into rings. Peel the oranges and cut into segments. Save the juice for the dressing if you wish.
2 Wash the watercress, tear into pieces and combine with the chicory and oranges.
3 Make the dressing and toss with the salad. Scatter with pine kernels.

EVERYDAY BREAD

Doris Grant's classic recipe is the basis for the bread I bake every day. I put no fat in it as the molasses helps to keep it from drying out too fast, and no salt. Because this bread contains no preservatives, it only lasts 3–4 days, but usually, it is eaten up long before then.

I always try to use English organically-grown, stoneground wholemeal flour, but this is not always practicable, since in a poor summer, the English wheat, even that grown on the sunny upland slopes of Wiltshire, does not produce a flour with enough gluten, which makes the bread soggy and difficult to bake. The only answer is to mix this flour with some harder flour from Canada.

I use the same flour for all my cooking, whether it be bread, pastry, cake or sauce and I find it suitable for all these purposes. 100% wholemeal flour does seem to absorb more water than white flour, but it is not difficult to adjust to this. One advantage is that when making bread with wholemeal flour, a lot of that time-consuming kneading is not necessary.

MAKES: 3 x 900g (2lb) loaves or 2 x 900g (2lb) loaves, plus 12 buns
PREPARATION TIME: approximately 2 hours
BAKING TIME: 25–30 minutes for buns
45–55 minutes for loaves

I heaped teaspoonful unsulphured blackstrap molasses
1.1 litres (2 pints) tepid water or milk or whey
2 teaspoonsful dried yeast
approximately 1.4kg (3 lb) stoneground 100 per cent wholemeal flour
butter to grease tins
poppy seeds, kibbled wheat or sesame seeds to sprinkle
(optional)

1 Put the molasses and water into a large mixing bowl and sprinkle in the yeast. After 10 minutes, the yeast should rise to the surface and be frothy. Mix in just enough flour using a balloon whisk to make a thick cream. Turn the oven on to its lowest point so that it is only just on, and put the bowl in the oven to prove. If the oven is too hot, it will kill the yeast.
2 Warm the bread or bun tins and grease with butter.
3 After 45 minutes, remove the bowl from the oven (the mixture should have swollen) but leave the oven on and add the flour in approximately 115g (4 oz) dollops, mixing it in thoroughly each time until you have a firmish dough. Take it out of the bowl, put on to a floured work surface and knead, adding a little more flour if necessary, until the dough

comes cleanly away from the work surface.

4 Divide the dough into loaves, roll the buns and place in the buttered tins. Brush a small patch on the top of each bun with water and sprinkle with poppy seeds, kibbled wheat or sesame seeds. Prove again in the warm oven. This should take 30 minutes to 1 hour.

5 Meanwhile, heat another oven to 400°F/200°C/Gas mark 6.

6 When the dough has risen level with the top of the tins it is ready for baking. Bake the buns for 25–30 minutes and the loaves for 45–55 minutes. When they are done, remove from the oven and leave the tins to stand for 5 minutes before lifting out the bread and/or buns onto a wire rack to cool.

Sometimes I vary the flavour and texture by using milk or whey instead of, or partly instead of, the water. This gives greater lightness to the bread, but it makes the top more likely to scorch.

BASIC BISCUITS

Nothing could be simpler than these biscuits. I have cut down the amount of sugar in this recipe and you could use even less, relying on the raisins for sweetening.

It is often possible to reduce the sugar content of a recipe. I always use unrefined sugar with the country of origin firmly stated on the packet. The word demerara denotes a type of sugar, not where it comes from. Billington's demerara, for instance, which I always use, comes from Mauritius. Unrefined sugar has far more strength of taste and character than refined sugar. It also contains valuable trace elements and minerals.

MAKES: approximately 16
PREPARATION TIME: 15 minutes
BAKING TIME: 12–15 minutes

115g (4 oz) unsalted butter
55g (2 oz) light muscovado sugar
85g (3 oz) raisins
few drips natural vanilla essence
200g (7 oz) wholemeal flour light, tasteless oil to grease
glacé cherries to decorate

1 Cream the butter and sugar together. Add the raisins, vanilla essence and work in the flour. I usually do this in a food processor.
2 Preheat the oven to 400°F/200°C/Gas mark 6.
3 Press the mixture firmly together and roll out on a cool work surface to a thickness of approximately .25cm (⅛-inch). Cut out desired shapes with a biscuit cutter dipped in a little additional flour and arrange on a well-oiled baking sheet. Decorate with glacé cherry quarters.
4 Bake for 12–15 minutes, until golden brown. Allow to cool slightly, then lift onto a wire rack to harden.

PUDDING THINS

These tiny biscuits are delicate and fragile, although they are made with wholemeal flour. They can be curled over a rolling pin while they are still warm from the oven and are a wonderful accompaniment to fruit creams, jellies, and sorbets.

MAKES: 20
COOKING TIME: 5 minutes
BAKING TIME: approximately 12 minutes

55g (2 oz) honey
55g (2 oz) unsalted butter
1–2 drops natural almond essence
55g (2 oz) wholemeal flour
butter to grease
chopped flaked almonds

1 Preheat the oven to 350°F/180°C/Gas mark 4.

2 Melt the honey and butter in a saucepan over a gentle heat. Remove from the heat and stir in the flour and almond essence. Mix well.

3 Drop a teaspoonful of the mixture onto a greased sheet, scatter over a few chopped flaked almonds and bake for approximately 12 minutes, until the biscuits turn light brown round the edges. Lift onto a wire rack to cool with a fish slice. Store in an airtight container.

WHOLEMEAL SHORTCRUST PASTRY

100 per cent wholemeal pastry need not be heavy and stodgy. The secret is to roll it out very thinly. An 85g (3 oz) amount is plenty for a tart base for 10–12 people. As well as being delicate in texture, the flavour is nutty and interesting.

PREPARATION TIME: 5 minutes

85g (3 oz) wholemeal flour
45g (1½ oz) cold unsalted butter
3 tablespoonful iced water
1 teaspoonful freshly grated Parmesan cheese and/or
sea salt and freshly ground black pepper (optional for
savoury pastry)
2 teaspoonful ground roasted nuts (optional for either
savoury or sweet pastry)
2 teaspoonful icing sugar or finely ground demerara sugar
(optional for sweet pastry)

1 Make the pastry in the bowl of an electric mixer or food processor. Sift the flour into the bowl and chop up the butter, which must be straight from the refrigerator. Mix at slow speed until it resembles fine breadcrumbs.
2 Add any of the optional extras, turn up the speed a notch and tip in the water. Watch until the pastry gathers itself up into a ball, then turn the motor off immediately.
3 Allow the pastry to rest at least 20 minutes before attempting to use it.
4 Roll out the pastry as thinly as possible on a cold, floured surface.

For a richer pastry, use 1 egg instead of water.

Baking Blind: After rolling out the pastry and fitting it into the dish, line the pastry with greaseproof paper and weigh down with old dried beans kept especially for that purpose. Make sure the beans fit right into the angle of the pastry – the object is to prevent the pastry from bulging in the wrong places. Bake for 10 minutes at 400°F/200°C/Gas mark 6, remove the beans and greaseproof paper, prick the base of the pastry lightly with a fork and bake for a further 5 minutes.

WHOLEMEAL PUFF PASTRY

This is a rich pastry made with wholemeal flour which melts in the mouth. It is not rolled out as thinly as shortcrust pastry, so one needs a little more of it.

PREPARATION TIME: 45 minutes
CHILLING TIME: 1 hour

200g (7 oz) wholemeal flour

200g (7 oz) cold unsalted butter

juice of ½ lemon

iced water

1 Put the flour in the bowl of an electric mixer or processor. Chop 55g (2 oz) of the butter directly from the refrigerator and mix into the flour on a low speed. Increase the speed slightly and add the lemon juice and a little iced water, 1 tablespoonful at a time, until the dough leaves the sides of the bowl and forms a ball. Stop the machine immediately, wrap the dough in cling film and chill in the refrigerator for 20 minutes.

2 Divide the remaining butter into three. Knock one third into a rectangle and roll out the pastry to approximately three times this size. Fold the bottom third up, place the butter on the top third and fold down. Press the edges together with a rolling pin, trying to trap some air in the envelope of dough. Turn the dough one quarter turn, roll into a rectangle again and using quick, short movements, repeat the folding and sealing. Wrap in cling film and refrigerate for 15 minutes.

3 Repeat the folding and sealing process twice more, using up the butter and trying always to incorporate as much air into the dough as possible. Refrigerate each time and keep chilled until ready for use.

RICH MOIST CHOCOLATE CAKE

Cakes made with 100% wholemeal flour have more body than those made with white flour and are far more satisfying. Spoil everyone with this cake on a special occasion. Make it at least one day in advance to allow it to moisten slightly.

Sandwich the layers together with Cinnamon Cream or a coffee butter cream and decorate with walnuts set in coffee icing, strewn with flaked chocolate.

MAKES: 1 x 20cm (8-inch) sandwich cake
PREPARATION TIME: 15 minutes plus decoration time
BAKING TIME: 20–25 minutes

	FILLING
light, tasteless oil to grease tins	
170g (6 oz) wholemeal flour plus flour to dust tins	Cinnamon Cream (page 124) or coffee butter cream
55g (2 oz) unsweetened cocoa powder	coffee icing
2 teaspoonsful baking powder	walnuts to decorate
225g (½ lb) unsalted butter	flaked chocolate to decorate
85g (3 oz) fine demerara sugar (see page 92)	
85g (3 oz) dark muscovado sugar	
4 free-range eggs, well-beaten	
I heaped teaspoonful unsulphured blackstrap molasses or honey	

1 Line the bottom of 2 x 20cm (8-inch) sandwich tins with baking parchment, brush the parchment and sides of the tins with oil and dust with flour, shaking out the excess.
2 Preheat the oven to 400°F/200°C/Gas mark 6.
3 Sift the flour with the cocoa and baking powder into a bowl. Cream the butter and sugar together in a large bowl until light and fluffy. Add the eggs alternately with the flour, mixing well after each addition. Finally, stir in the molasses or honey.
4 Divide the mixture evenly between the two prepared cake tins and bake in the centre of the oven for 20–25 minutes, until the cakes have risen and the centres spring back when lightly touched. Allow to cool in the tins for 5 minutes, then turn out onto a wire rack and carefully peel off the paper.
5 When the cakes are completely cold, sandwich together with Cinnamon Cream or a coffee butter cream. Ice the sides and top with a coffee icing and decorate with walnuts and flaked chocolate.

BROWN BREAD ICE CREAM

This gorgeous ice cream has been rediscovered in recent years – the Victorians and Edwardians were mad about it – and it has almost become a cliché, but I make no apologies for including it in any list of favourites.

SERVES: 10–12
BAKING TIME: 30 minutes
PREPARATION TIME: 10 minutes
COOKING TIME: 10 minutes
FREEZING TIME: 6–8 hours

225g (8oz) wholemeal breadcrumbs
175g (6oz) dark muscovado sugar
285ml (½ pint) fresh milk
4 egg yolks
570ml (1 pint) fresh double cream
60ml (2 fl oz) light rum

1 Preheat the oven to 400°F/200°C/Gas mark 6.

2 Mix the breadcrumbs and sugar briefly in a processor and tip onto a large open tin. Toast them in the oven for about 30 minutes, turning often with a fork. The mixture should be set and crisp. Remove from the oven and leave to cool. Break up the bigger lumps with a rolling pin or process briefly.

3 Scald the milk in a saucepan. Beat the egg yolks in a bowl. Pour the milk into the egg yolks in a steady stream, mixing well. Return to the rinsed out saucepan and cook over a low heat, whisking well until a thick custard is formed. Set aside until cold.

4 Whip the cream lightly and stir in the rum. Fold into the cold custard and combine with the breadcrumbs. Freeze in a covered container until firm, about 6–8 hours. There is no need to beat this mixture when it is half-frozen.

YORKSHIRE CURD TART

Yorkshire has given its name to so many good things to eat and this cheese cake in one very good example. I always enjoy serving it – it is surprising how many of our visitors have Yorkshire connections. The pastry should be as thin as possible and the filling should be deep and generous.

MAKES: 1 x 22.5cm (9-inch) tart
PREPARATION TIME: making the pastry,
plus 10 minutes
RESTING TIME: 20 minutes
BAKING TIME: 30 minutes

PASTRY

85g (3 oz) wholemeal flour
45g (1½ oz) lard
3 tablespoonsful natural yogurt

FILLING

85g (3 oz) unsalted butter
55g (2 oz) golden granulated sugar
340g (¾ lb) curd (see page 42)
115g (4 oz) raisins
1 tablespoonful wholemeal breadcrumbs
freshly grated nutmeg
2 large free-range eggs, beaten
fresh thick Jersey cream to serve

1 Make the pastry in the usual manner (see page 176) and allow to rest for 20 minutes. Use to line a 23cm (9-inch) tart tin with removable base.
2 Preheat the oven to 425°F/220°C/Gas mark 7.
3 Cream the butter and sugar together. Stir in the curd, raisins and breadcrumbs. Grate in enough nutmeg for your taste, then mix in the eggs.
4 Pour the curd mixture into the pastry case and bake for 30 minutes. The top should puff up and brown.
5 Eat hot or cold with a little more nutmeg grated over the top and thick Jersey cream. In more clement weather, this is a very good pudding to take on picnics.

DAMSON CUSTARD TART

Damsons, their bloom as blue as Housman's 'blue remembered hills', have a rich and sharp intensity, which has made them a favoured fruit for conserves, pickles, jellies and wines. Damsons are ideal for sauces and to enliven custards, milk puddings and strong ice creams. An attractive alternative fruit for this tart is the black Morello cherry, which cooks to a wonderful crimson.

MAKES: 1 x 22.5cm (9-inch) tart
PREPARATION TIME: making the pastry, baking blind, plus approximately 10 minutes
COOKING TIME: 15-20 minutes
BAKING TIME: 20 minutes

I recipe quantity wholemeal shortcrust pastry made with fine demerara sugar (see page 92)
900g (2 lb) damsons
2 tablespoonsful water
I tablespoonful demerara sugar

CUSTARD

2 egg yolks
140ml (¼ pint) fresh double cream
I tablespoonful demerara sugar
½ teaspoon ground cinnamon
few drops natural vanilla essence
fresh thick Jersey cream to serve

1 Line a 22.5cm (9-inch) fluted flan tin with a removable base with the pastry and bake blind according to the instructions on page 176.
2 Preheat the oven to 350°F/180°C/Gas mark 4.
3 Put the damsons and water in a saucepan and simmer slowly for 15–20 minutes, until soft. Pick out as many stones as you can. Sweeten to taste and put into a pastry case.
4 Whizz all the custard ingredients together in a liquidizer, then pour over the damsons, making sure that some of the damsons are showing through.
5 Bake for 20 minutes until the custard is set and lightly browned. Serve with thick cream.

MAIDS OF HONOUR OR RICHMOND CAKES

These delectable little almond cakes are reputed to have been offered by Henry VIII to his wives. They are so-named because the Maids of Honour at Court were sent across the river to Richmond to collect them from the bakery where they were made. Queen Elizabeth I is said to have enjoyed them too – noble recommendations! I bake them in brioche tins, which give a pretty fluted effect.

MAKES 6–7

PREPARATION TIME: making the pastry,
plus 20 minutes
BAKING TIME: 20 minutes

FILLING

115g (4 oz) whole almonds blanched (see below)
55g (2 oz) unsalted butter
85g (3 oz) fine demerara sugar (see page 92)
1 teaspoonful wholemeal flour
2 egg yolks, beaten
grated zest of 1 well scrubbed lemon
juice of ½ lemon
55g (2 oz) curd
few drops natural almond essence (optional)
approximately 3 tablespoonful quince, medlar
or damson jelly or jam
light, tasteless oil for the moulds
1 recipe quantity wholemeal shortcrust pastry, made
with 1 teaspoon icing sugar, 1 egg yolk and
1 tablespoonful cold water
fresh thick Jersey cream to serve (optional)

1 Put the almonds in a bowl. Blanch by pouring hot water over them. After a few minutes the skins should rub off easily. Grind the almonds in a processor.
2 Cream the butter and sugar until light and fluffy. Add the flour, egg yolks, lemon zest and juice, curd and ground almonds. If the mixture does not taste almondy enough, add a few drops of almond essence.
3 Preheat the oven to 400°F/200°C/Gas mark 6. Put a baking sheet into the oven to heat.
4 Roll out the pastry and use to line well-oiled brioche moulds. Put a dob of jelly or jam in

the bottom of each pastry case. Fill with the almond mixture and bake on the preheated baking sheet for 20 minutes, until the filling has risen and turned golden.

5 These are lovely served on their own, even better with thick Jersey cream.

APPLE PIE

Apples must be the most loved and prized fruit in the English kitchen garden. Old cookery books are full of recipes for cooking pippins, costards and codlins in puddings, pies, chutneys, conserves and meat dishes, and their varied colour and flavour can be appreciated from August to April.

SERVES: 6
PREPARATION TIME: making the pastry
plus 15 minutes
COOKING TIME: 20 minutes
COOLING TIME: 30 minutes
BAKING TIME: 20 minutes

900g (2 lb) Bramley apples
85g (3 oz) raisins
juice and grated zest of 1 well scrubbed lemon
2–3 whole cloves
½ teaspoonful ground cinnamon
285ml (½ pint) dry cider
2 free-range eggs, well-beaten
55–85g (2–3 oz) light muscovado sugar
1 recipe quantity Wholemeal Puff Pastry made with
1 teaspoonful icing sugar (page 177)
fresh thick Jersey cream

1 Peel and core the apples and put them in a saucepan with all the remaining ingredients, except for the eggs and sugar. Stew them over a moderate heat until soft and puffy. If the pulp is too loose, strain off the juice and reduce to a syrup before mixing it back into the apples. Allow to cool slightly, then mix in the eggs and sugar. Put into a 1 litre (1½ pint) pie dish and allow to cool thoroughly.
2 Preheat the oven to 400°F/200°C/Gas mark 6.
3 Roll out the pastry thinly to cover the dish. When the apple mixture is cool, fit on the pastry lid, cut two holes in the top to allow the steam to escape and decorate with shapes from the pastry trimmings. Bake for 20 minutes until the pastry has risen and become golden-brown.
4 Serve hot with thick Jersey cream. A lovely North Country custom is to serve a wedge of cheese such as Wensleydale with apple pie.

APPLE, QUINCE AND HONEY SUET CRUST

This is a marvellous dish for the colder months and is a light version of the traditional suet pudding. Only 85g (3 oz) of suet is used for the pastry, which is finely rolled and filled with plenty of fruit. The pastry is too fragile to support the filling if it were to be turned out, so I just cut wedges out of the bowl.

The quince turns a delightful coral-pink when it is cooked and imparts an indescribable fragrance, which wafts from the basin when the lid is lifted. Quinces, like apples, overwinter well if stored in a cool place. They can also be sliced and frozen quite successfully.

I find a boilable plastic 1 litre (2-pint) pudding basin with a snap-on lid indispensable and very practical for steamed puddings, if more mundane than the traditional china bowl and cotton cloth, complete proof against sogginess. Baked custard is the natural and perfect accompaniment for steamed puddings (see page 48).

SERVES: 6

PREPARATION TIME: 20–30 minutes

RESTING TIME: 30 minutes

COOKING TIME: 3 hours

PASTRY	FILLING
85g (3 oz) fresh beef suet	455g (1 lb) cooking apples
170g (6 oz) wholemeal flour	1 large, ripe quince
2–3 tablespoonsful iced water	4 heaped tablespoonsful honey
	pinch of powdered ginger
	3 whole cloves

1 First make the pastry. Use the processor to grate the suet. Add the flour, whizz for a moment and then add the water. As soon as the pastry is amalgamated and leaves the sides of the bowl, stop the machine. Leave the pastry to rest for at least 30 minutes.

2 Peel, core and slice the apples and quince. Roll out the pastry fairly thinly. Put a dollop of honey in the bottom of a 1 litre (2-pint) pudding basin and line the basin with some of the pastry, making sure you have enough left over for the lid. Fill with layers of fruit, honey and spices. Re-roll the pastry for the lid and fit it on the pudding. Snap on the basin lid and steam steadily in a covered saucepan for at least 3 hours. Keep topping up the water from a boiling kettle and make sure the water never stops boiling or drops below halfway point.

3 Serve steaming hot with baked custard or cream.

SIX CUP PUDDING

This is an adaptation of Alison Uttley's recipe. I have substituted apricots for currants and used honey instead of sugar to make a really opulent steamed pudding. I use teacups as my measure.

SERVES: 6
PREPARATION TIME: 10 minutes
COOKING TIME: 3 hours

I teacup wholemeal flour
I ½ teaspoonsful baking powder
I teacup unsalted butter
I teacup sun-dried unsulphured apricots
I teacup raisins
I egg, made up to I teacup with milk
extra butter to grease the mould
I teacup honey
Custard Sauce (page 187) or
fresh thick Jersey cream to serve

1 Using an electric mixer or food processor, work the flour, baking powder and butter to a crumble. Add the apricots and raisins and lastly, the milk and egg.
2 Put one-third of the honey in the bottom of a greased 1 litre (2-pint) boilable plastic pudding basin with a snap-on lid. Fill the basin with the fruit mixture, putting another third of the honey in the centre and the remainder on top. Snap on the lid and steam steadily in enough boiling water to come halfway up the sides of the basin in a covered saucepan for at least 3 hours. Keep topping up the water from a boiling kettle.
3 Turn the pudding out onto a heated serving dish and serve with hot Custard Sauce (page 187) or thick Jersey cream.

CUSTARD SAUCE

Real instant custard! What could be more English? Perfect with fresh fruit or incorporated into trifles and brûlées, elevated with cream or lightened with milk, the base of so many ice creams and puddings.

MAKES: approximately 285ml (½ pint)
PREPARATION TIME: minimal
COOKING TIME: 10–15 minutes

4 egg yolks
I tablespoonful demerara sugar
I vanilla pod or natural vanilla essence
285ml (½ pint) fresh milk

1 Beat the egg yolks in a bowl with the sugar.
2 Heat the milk with the vanilla pod, if you are using one, over a gentle heat. Extract the vanilla pod, which can be rinsed and dried and used again, and pour over the eggs and sugar, whisking well. Return to the cleaned saucepan and add 1–2 drops of vanilla essence to taste if necessary. Keep whisking over a gentle heat until the custard becomes creamy and thick. Do not allow the custard to become too hot or it will curdle.

If disaster does occur and the custard curdles, remedial measures are: take the pan off the heat and beat in another egg yolk, or whisk in an ice cube.

CHESTNUT, CHOCOLATE AND PRUNE PUDDING

I was once told that this was 'the nearest thing to a savoury pudding'!

SERVES: 6
COOKING TIME: 10 minutes the day before,
plus 1 hour
SOAKING TIME: overnight
PREPARATION TIME: 30 minutes

9 large unsorbated Californian prunes (18–24 if possible)
Darjeeling tea (optional)
170g (6 oz) dried chestnuts
1 vanilla pod
2 tablespoonsful honey
85g (3 oz) strong, bitter chocolate
2 tablespoonsful hot water
fresh whipped cream to decorate
marrons glacé (optional)

1 The day before, simmer the prunes in a saucepan with Darjeeling tea or water for 10 minutes. Remove from the heat and leave to swell. Put the chestnuts into a bowl, cover with water and allow to soak overnight.

2 On the day, drain the chestnuts, cook them with 425ml (¾ pint) water and the vanilla pod over a moderate heat until the chestnuts will crumble easily, about 45 minutes. Remove the vanilla pod, drain the chestnuts, reserving the cooking liquor and process with the honey; the consistency should be fairly stiff. Correct with the reserved cooking liquid if necessary.

3 Melt the chocolate in a bowl over hot water. Add 2 tablespoons of hot water and stir until smooth.

4 Drain the prunes, halve lengthways and stone.

5 To serve, put a spoonful of chestnut purée in the centre of each plate and arrange a trefoil of 3 prune halves, cut side in, sloping up against the chestnuts. Coat the backs of the prunes with the melted chocolate and decorate with a finial of whipped cream and some crumbled marrons glacés to spoil your guests.

WINTER MENUS

SIMPLE SUPPER

Shallot and Parsley Soup (page 142)

Thatched Cottage Pie (page 163)
Broccoli
Carrots

Rich moist Chocolate Cake (page 178) or Fresh Fruit

VEGETARIAN SUPPER OR LIGHT LUNCH

Cardoon Boats (page 149)

Sunset Beans (page 169)
Curly Kale
Leeks
Haut-Baked Potatoes (page 26)

Brown Bread Ice Cream (page 179)

DINNER PARTY

Scallops in Saffron and Yogurt Sauce (page 156)

Salmi of Wild Duck (page 160)
Red Cabbage and Apple (page 168)
Purée of Swedes
Gratin Potatoes (page 27)

Celery and Grape Salad (page 120)

Six Cup Pudding (page 186) with Custard Sauce (page 187)
Chestnut, Chocolate and Prune Pudding (page 188)